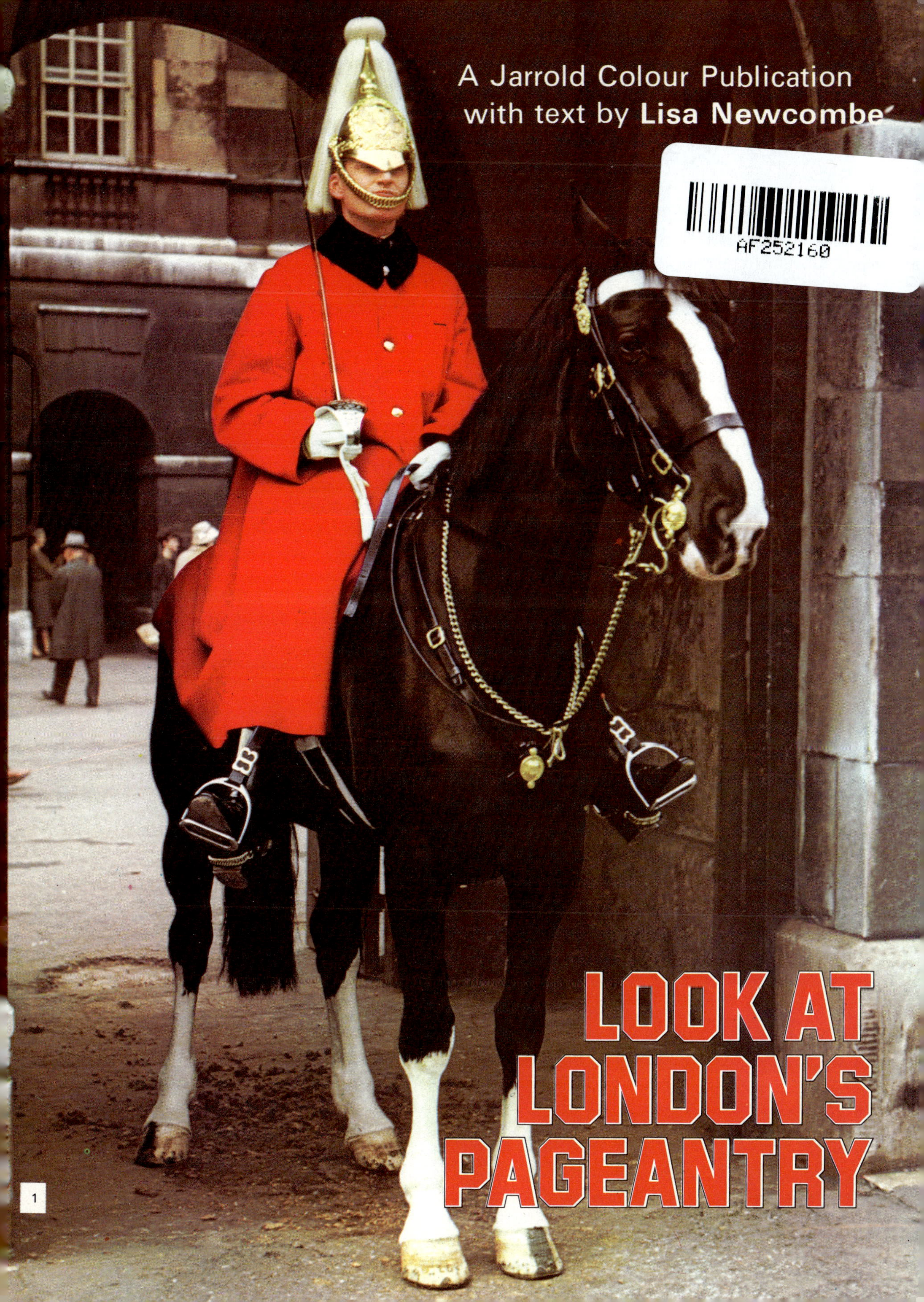

A Jarrold Colour Publication
with text by Lisa Newcombe
AF252160
LOOK AT
LONDON'S
PAGEANTRY

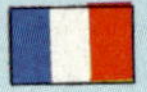

LISTE DES PHOTOGRAPHIES

1. *Sentinelle à cheval des gardes du corps.*
2. *Extérieur de la Cathédrale St Paul.*
3. *L'orchestre du corps des grenadiers.*
4. *Parade du Lord Maire, avec son carrosse doré.*
5. *Le Chancelier du Palais de Westminster.*
6. *Big Ben et les Chambres du Parlement.*
7. *La chambre des Communes.*
8. *La chambre des Lords.*
9. *Le carrosse d'Etat à l'ouverture du Parlement.*
10. *Sa Majesté la Reine dans son carrosse.*
11. *Le chœur de l'Abbaye de Westminster.*
12. *Les tours-ouest de l'abbaye de Westminster.*
13. *Mariage de la Princesse Anne à Westminster.*
14. *Le cénotaphe, monument de guerre à Whitehall.*
15. *Relève des gardes à cheval.*
16. *Les gardes à cheval de la cavalerie royale.*
17. *Les gardes du corps à la cour du Horse Guards.*
18. *La cérémonie annuelle du « défilé des drapeaux ».*
19. *La reine au « défilé des drapeaux ».*
20. *Le défilé, point culminant de la cérémonie.*
21. *La façade imposante du Palais du Buckingham.*
22. *Un orchestre des gardes à pied dans le Mall.*
23. *Les gardes à cheval de la cavalerie royale.*
24. *Gardes du régiment des Coldstream.*
25. *L'orchestre de l'artillerie royale dans le Mall.*
26. *Un orchestre des gardes au Palais de Buckingham.*
27. *Joueurs de trompette de la cavalerie royale.*
28. *Représantants des régiments de l'infanterie.*
29. *Relève de la garde au palais de Buckingham.*
30. *Un détachement des gardes du corps dans le Mall.*
31. *La Tour de Londres.*
32. *Les gardiens « yeoman » de la Tour de Londres.*
33. *Cérémonie du « battement des bornes » à la Tour.*
34. *Le défi, la cérémonie des clefs à la Tour.*
35. *Le gardien principal en habit de cérémonie.*
36. *La cérémonie des clefs à la Tour.*
37. *L'artillerie faisant feu au pont de la Tour.*
38. *L'un des six corbeaux de la Tour de Londres.*
39. *Deux gardiens appelés les « Beefeaters ».*
40. *« Jour du Fondateur » à l'hôpital royal, Chelsea.*
41. *Un retraité de l'hôpital royal, Chelsea.*
42. *Représentants de la cavalerie royale.*
43. *« Cicero », portant les tambours de la cavalerie.*
44. *Les troupes montées royales.*
45. *Un « pearly king » avec son complet de boutons.*
46. *Le défilé des chevaux à charrette à Regent's Park.*
47. *Le défilé de Pâques à Battersea Park.*
48. *Vue aérienne du château de Windsor.*
49. *Défilé de l'Ordre de la Jarretière à Windsor.*
50. *Cérémonie de la Jarretière, Chapelle St George.*

BILDERVERZEICHNIS

1. *Ein Leibgardist auf seinem Pferd.*
2. *Das Außere der St. Pauls Kathedrale.*
3. *Die Musik des Grenadiergardekorps.*
4. *Der Festzug des Lord Mayor.*
5. *Der Großkanzler im Westminster Palast.*
6. *„Big Ben" und das Parlamentsgebäude.*
7. *Die Kammer des Unterhauses.*
8. *Die Kammer des Oberhauses.*
9. *Die Staatskutsche bei der Eröffnung.*
10. *Ihre Majestät die Königin in ihrer Kutsche.*
11. *Der Chor in der Westminster Abtei.*
12. *Die beiden Westtürme der Abtei.*
13. *Die Hochzeit der Prinzessin Anne in der Abtei.*
14. *Das Zenotaph, das Londoner Ehrendenkmal.*
15. *Die Gardekavallerie löst die Wache ab.*
16. *Die königliche Gardekavallerie.*
17. *Leibgardisten auf dem Horse Guards Hof.*
18. *Die jährliche Fahnenparade „Trooping the Colour".*
19. *Die Königin bei der Fahnenparade.*
20. *Die Regimente der Garde marschieren vorbei.*
21. *Die imposante Fassade des Buckingham Palasts.*
22. *Die Musik des Gardekorps auf dem Mall.*
23. *Die königliche Gardekavallerie.*
24. *Soldaten des Coldstreamgardekorps.*
25. *Die Musik-Kapelle der königlichen Artillerie.*
26. *Die Musik-Kapelle des Gardekorps verläßt den Palast.*
27. *Trompeter der königlichen Kavallerie.*
28. *Soldaten aus jedem Regiment des Gardekorps.*
29. *Die Wachablösung vor Buckingham Palast.*
30. *Eine Abteilung Leibgardisten auf dem Mall.*
31. *Der Tower of London.*
32. *Die „Yeoman warders" bewachen den Tower.*
33. *Die Zeremonie „Beating the Bounds" im Tower.*
34. *Das Rufen „Wer da?" bei der Schlüsselzeremonie.*
35. *Der Hauptwächter in feierlicher Uniform.*
36. *Die Schlüsselzeremonie im Tower.*
37. *Die Artillerie schießen Salut.*
38. *Einer der sechs Raben im Tower.*
39. *Zwei „Yeoman Warders", auch „Beefeaters" genannt.*
40. *Stiftertag im Königlichen Hospital, Chelsea.*
41. *Ein „Chelsea Pensioner", alter Soldat.*
42. *Ein Offizier und ein Trompeter der Kavallerie.*
43. *„Cicero", Trommelpferd der Leibwache.*
44. *Die königliche Truppe der Artillerie.*
45. *Ein „Perlenkönig".*
46. *Die Lastpferdeparade im Regent's Park.*
47. *Die Osterparade im Battersea Park.*
48. *Eine Luftaufnahme von dem.*
49. *Die Hosenbandordenparade am Schloß Windsor.*
50. *Die Hosenbandordenzeremonie, Windsor.*

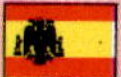

LISTA DE FOTOGRAFIAS

1. *Centinela a caballo de la Guardia de Corps.*
2. *Exterior de la Catedral de San Pablo.*
3. *La Banda de los Granaderos de la Guardia.*
4. *Parada del Lord Alcalde con su dorada carroza.*
5. *El Canciller en el Palacio de Westminster.*
6. *« Big Ben » y las Casas del Parlamento.*
7. *La Cámara de los Comunes.*
8. *La Cámara de los Lores.*
9. *La Carroza Real a la apertura del Parlamento.*
10. *Su Majestad la Reina en su Carroza.*
11. *El Coro de la Abadía de Westminster.*
12. *Torres Occidentales — Abadía de Westminster.*
13. *Nupcias de la Princesa Ana en Westminster.*
14. *El Cenotafio, memorial de guerra en Whitehall.*
15. *El relevo de la Guardia Montada.*
16. *Jinetes de la Escolta Real.*
17. *Guardas de Corps en el Patio de Caballerías.*
18. *Ceremonia anual del « Desfile de las Banderas ».*
19. *La Reina revista el « Desfile de las Banderas ».*
20. *El desfile, punto culminante de la ceremonia.*
21. *Imponente fachada del Palacio de Buckingham.*
22. *Una Banda de Infantería de la Guardia Real.*
23. *Jinetes de la Escolta Real.*
24. *Centinelas de la Guardia de Coldstream.*
25. *La Banda de la Artillería Real en el Mall.*
26. *Una Banda de Guardias saliendo del Palacio.*
27. *Los Trompetas de la Escolta Real.*
28. *Soldados de cada Cuerpo de Guardas de a Pie.*
29. *El relevo de la Guardia en el Palacio.*
30. *Destacamento de Guardas de Corps en el Mall.*
31. *La Torre de Londres.*
32. *Alabarderos custodiando la Torre de Londres.*
33. *Ceremonia « Batida de los Lindes » en la Torre.*
34. *El « ¡Alto! » — Ceremonia de las Llaves.*
35. *El Jefe Alabardero en traje de Gala.*
36. *La « Ceremonia de las Llaves » en la Torre.*
37. *Salva de Artillería por le Puente de la Torre.*
38. *Uno de los seis cuervos de la Torre de Londres.*
39. *Dos Alabarderos o « Beefeaters ».*
40. *« Día del Fundador » en el Hospital Real, Chelsea.*
41. *Un típico veterano jubilado de Chelsea.*
42. *Un Oficial y un Trompeta de la Escolta Real.*
43. *« Cicero », Caballo-Tambor de la Escolta Real.*
44. *« La Tropa del Rey », Real Artillería Montada.*
45. *Rey Perlino en traje de botones nacarados.*
46. *La Parada de Caballos de Tiro en Regent's Park.*
47. *La Parada de Pascua en el Parque de Battersea.*
48. *Vista aérea del Castillo de Windsor.*
49. *Procesión de la Orden de la Jarretera, en Windsor.*
50. *Investidura de la Jarretera, Windsor.*

LISTA DELLE ILLUSTRAZIONI

1. *Una sentinella delle Life Guards a cavallo.*
2. *L'esterno della Cattedrale di S. Paolo.*
3. *La banda dei Granatieri.*
4. *La sfilata del Lord Mayor con il cocchio dorato.*
5. *Il Cancelliere al Palazzo di Westminster.*
6. *Big Ben ed il Parlamento.*
7. *La sala del consiglio al Palazzo dei Comuni.*
8. *La sala del consiglio al Palazzo dei Lords.*
9. *Il Cocchio reale all'apertura del Parlamento.*
10. *La Regina nella sua carozza.*
11. *Il coro dell'Abbazia di Westminster.*
12. *Le torri occidentali dell'Abbazia di Westminster.*
13. *Le nozze della Principessa Anna a Westminster.*
14. *Il Cenotafio in Whitehall commemorante le guerre.*
15. *Il cambio della Guardia.*
16. *Le guardie della Cavalleria Reale.*
17. *Life Guards nella spianata di Horse Guards.*
18. *L'annuale rivista militare.*
19. *La Regina alla Parata Militare.*
20. *L'apogeo della Parata Militare.*
21. *L'imponente facciata di Buckingham Palace.*
22. *La banda della fanteria nel Mall.*
23. *Guardie della Cavalleria reale.*
24. *Corazzieri del reggimento Coldstream.*
25. *La banda della Artiglieria Reale nel Mall.*
26. *La banda delle guardie a Buckingham Palace.*
27. *Trombettieri della Cavalleria Reale.*
28. *Componenti dei vari reggimenti di fanteria.*
29. *Il cambio della guardia a Buckingham Palace.*
30. *Un distaccamento delle Life Guards nel Mall.*
31. *La Torre di Londra.*
32. *Yeoman, la tipica guardia della Torre.*
33. *Annuale cerimonia alla Torre: « Beating the Bounds ».*
34. *Il chi-va-là, cerimonia delle chiavi.*
35. *Il capo yeoman nell'uniforme da cerimonia.*
36. *La cerimonia delle chiavi alla Torre.*
37. *Saluto a salve dell'Artiglieria a Tower Bridge.*
38. *Uno dei sei famosi corvi della Torre.*
39. *Due Yeoman sopranominati « Beefeaters ».*
40. *Giornata del Fondatore dell'Ospizio Reale, Chelsea.*
41. *Un tipico pensionante dell'Ospizio Reale, Chelsea.*
42. *Ufficiale e trombettiere della Cavalleria Reale.*
43. *« Cicero », cavallo porta tamburo della Cavalleria.*
44. *La parata del Re dell'artiglieria a Cavallo.*
45. *Il caratteristico costume del Re di Madreperla.*
46. *La sfilata dei cavalli da tiro a Regent's Park.*
47. *La Processione Pasquale al Parco di Battersea.*
48. *Veduta aerea del Castello di Windsor.*
49. *Sfilata dell'Ordine della Giarrettiera a Windsor.*
50. *Cerimoniale dell'Ordine della Giarrettiera.*

The City

St Paul's Cathedral is the third church to stand on this Ludgate Hill site in the City of London. A Saxon one was situated here first and then the medieval cathedral which was destroyed in 1666 in the Great Fire of London. This terrible holocaust, however, was to ultimately benefit London, as it led to the introduction of the English Renaissance. The greatest architect of the Renaissance was Sir Christopher Wren and St Paul's Cathedral, begun in 1675, is undoubtedly his masterpiece (2). The exterior of St Paul's is classical in style and its great dome, 365 feet high, is surmounted by a golden ball and cross. The vast interior contains such glories as Grinling Gibbons's choir stalls and the famous Whispering Gallery. In the Crypt are the tombs of Nelson, Wellington and Wren himself. As befits its status as England's largest Protestant church, the many services held in St Paul's are magnificent, especially the Carol Services at Christmas. St Paul's is also famous for its choir (the choir boys are taught at its own school), while its massive organ is probably the finest in the country. Many notable performances are given by the cathedral choir, including Handel's 'Messiah' at Advent and Bach's Saint Matthew Passion at Easter. Outside St Paul's, among the surrounding modern office blocks, the visitor is sometimes fortunate enough to hear a rousing performance by the band of the Grenadier Guards (3). Of all the pageants that London has to offer, the Lord Mayor's Show is one of the most popular. This takes place each year on the second Saturday in November, in honour of the newly elected Lord Mayor of London. In its early form (for this custom of fêting the Lord Mayor began about 600 years ago) a procession of state barges carried the Mayor up the Thames, but nowadays he rides in a magnificent gilded coach which weighs four tons and is drawn by six horses (4). It was built in 1757 from a design chosen by Sir William Chambers and its panels were painted by the Florentine artist Giovanni Cipriani. The coach is accompanied by a bodyguard of the Company of Pikemen and Musketeers, dressed in half-armour, and by Beadles, also wearing their traditional costumes, and it is preceded by a gay procession of floats carrying tableaux which depict aspects of London's life and history. The Lord Mayor and his entourage set out from Guildhall, pass St Paul's Cathedral and then proceed down Fleet Street to the Royal Courts of Justice in the Strand, where the Mayor takes his oath of office. He then returns to Guildhall for the Lord Mayor's Banquet in the evening (famous for its turtle soup), which is attended by the Prime Minister, the previous Lord Mayor, and many other dignitaries.

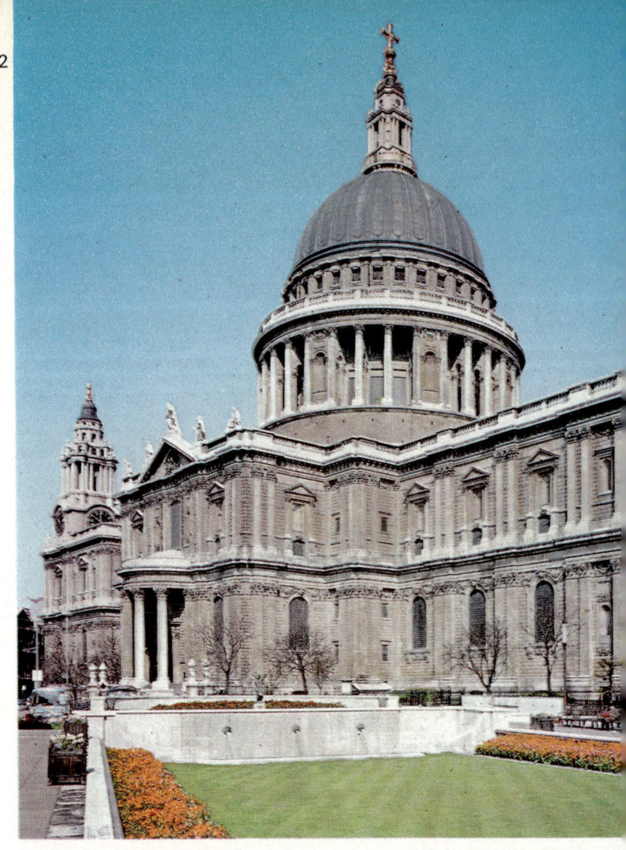

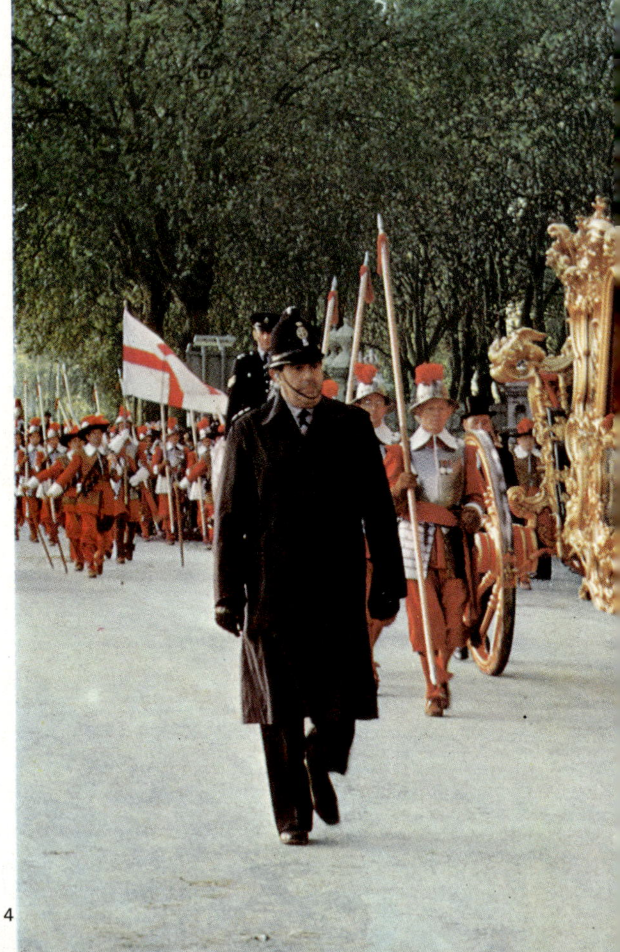

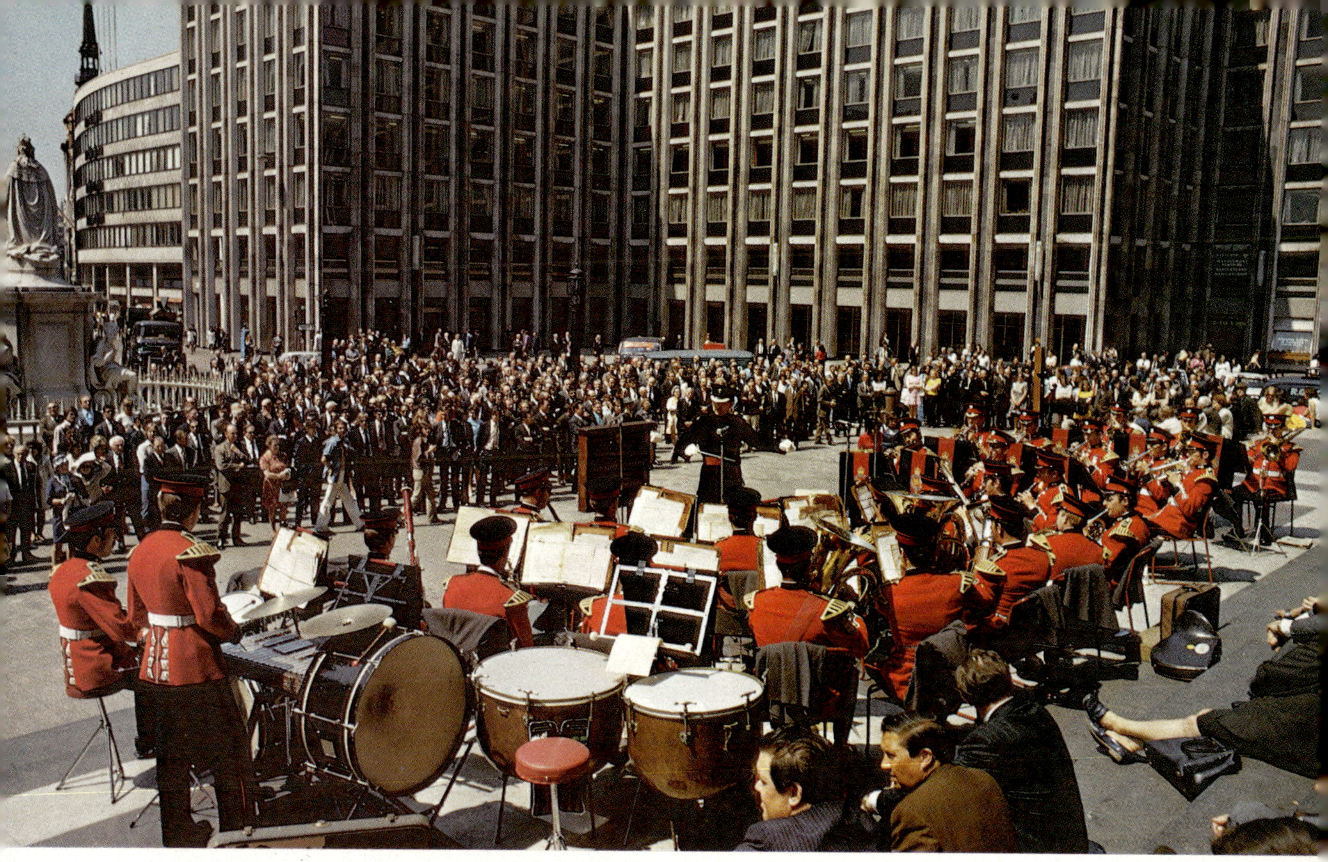

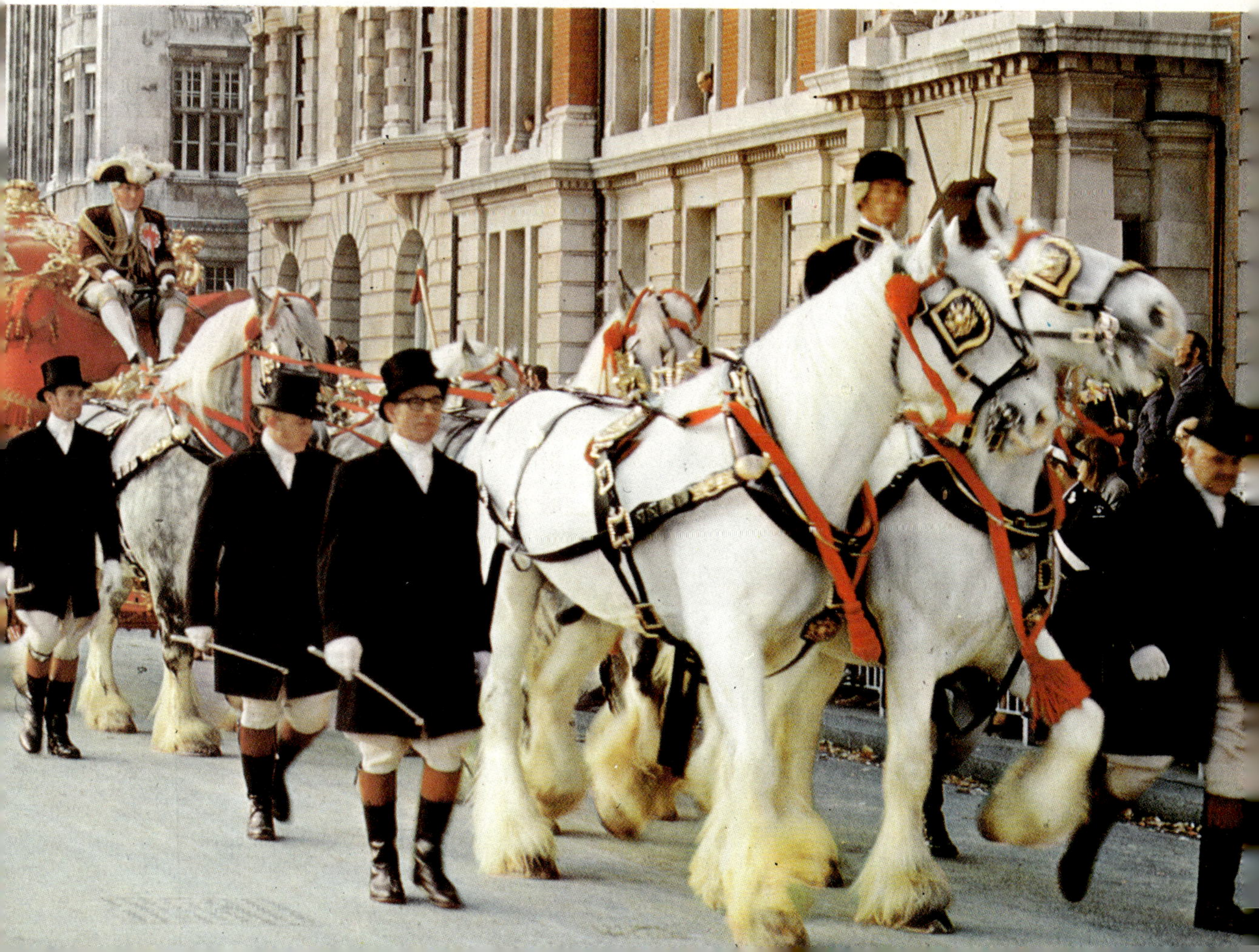

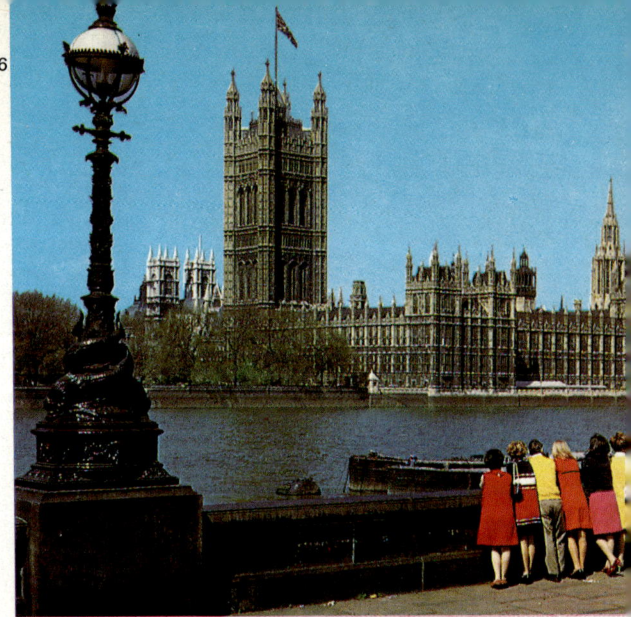

The Houses of Parliament

The Houses of Parliament (6) are the seat of our national legislature and, as such, are the scene of much of London's most impressive pageantry. The Lord Chancellor is shown here (5) at the Opening of the Legal Year, for instance, while each Parliamentary session involves a strict, traditional protocol. In the Chamber of the House of Commons (7) the Speaker presides from his Chair while Members of the Government sit on his right, and the Opposition on his left. Any Member who crosses the Floor must first bow to the Speaker's Chair. The Chamber of the House of Lords (8) is even more awe-inspiring. Here, the Lord Chancellor presides as Speaker and he sits on the Woolsack, an ottoman stuffed with wool which was originally adopted as a reminder of the importance of the English wool trade. At the Opening of Parliament, in November, the Queen arrives in the Irish State Coach (9) and is met by the Law Lords. She then dons the Parliament Robe and the Imperial State Crown, and enters the House of Lords. Now the Gentleman Usher of the Black Rod proceeds to the House of Commons, knocks three times with his Rod, and demands that 'This Honourable House' should attend the House of Lords. The returning procession is led by the Serjeant at Arms and the Speaker and, when all are assembled, the Queen delivers her speech.

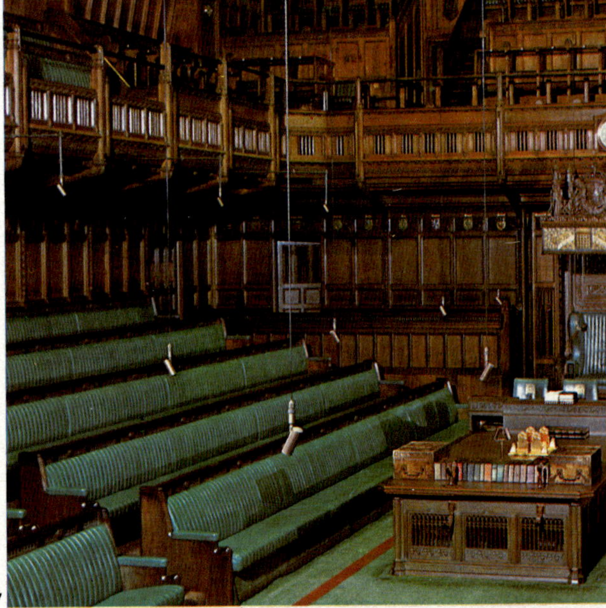

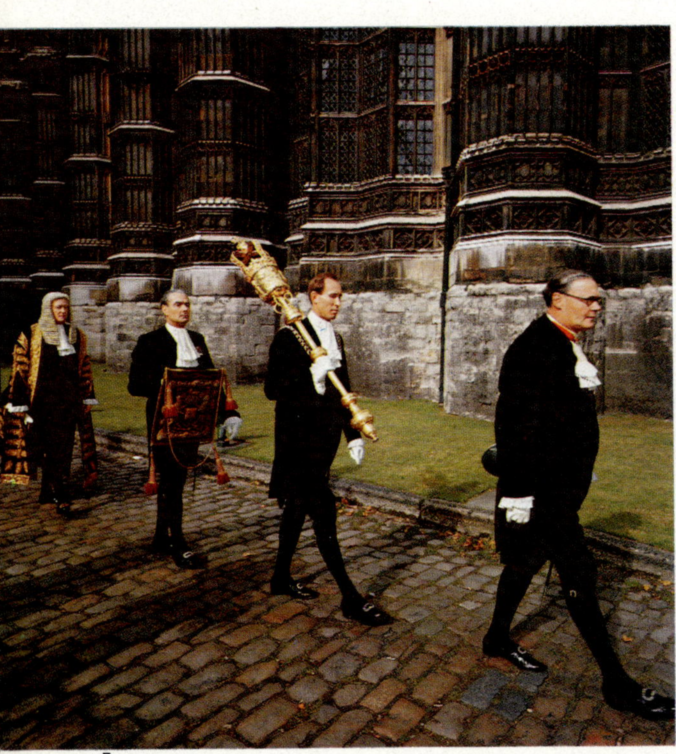

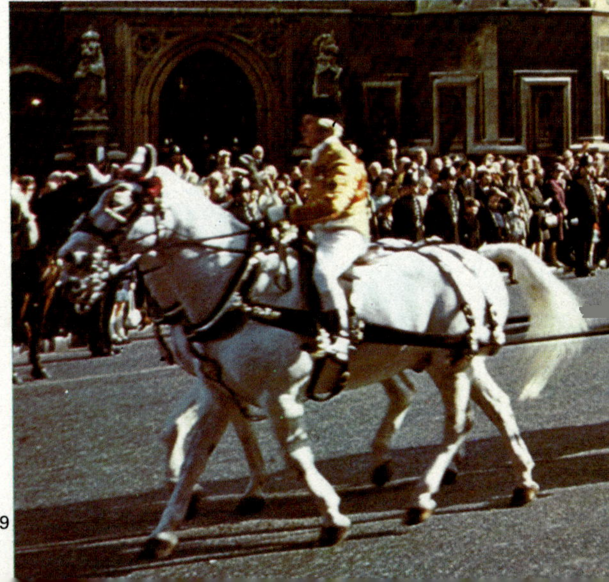

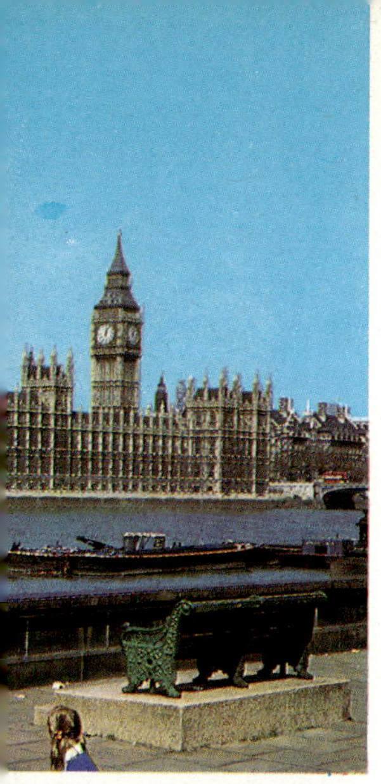

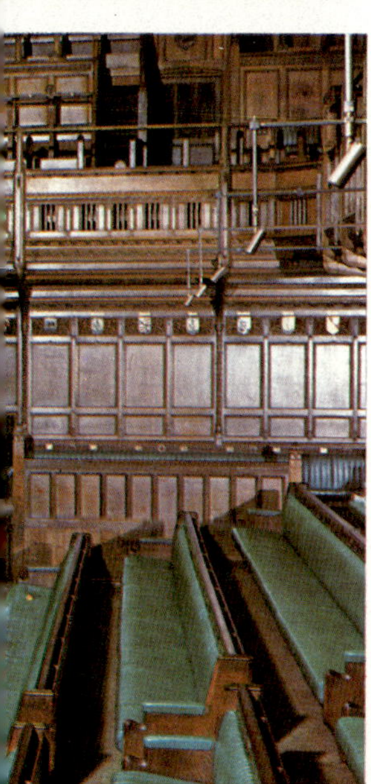

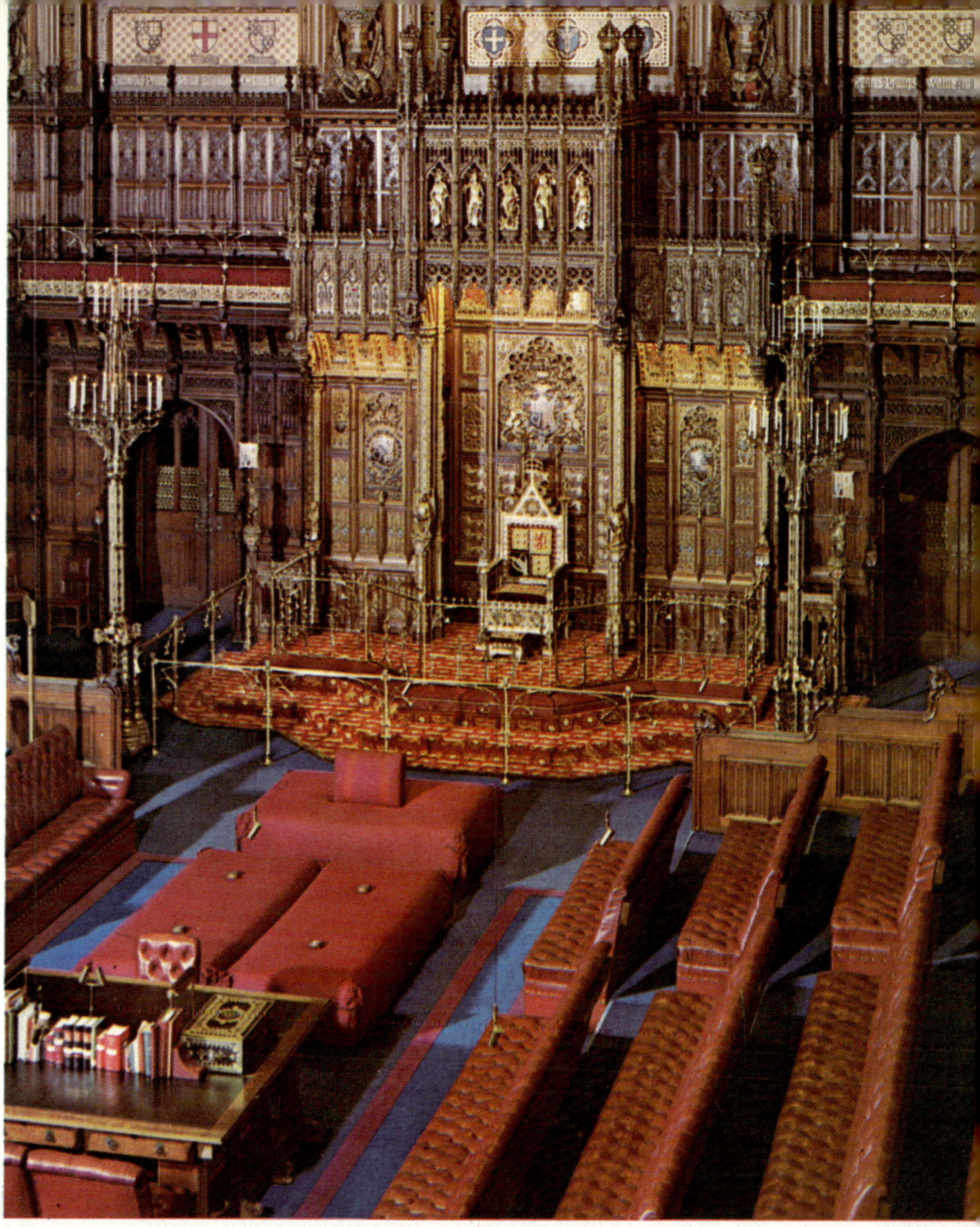

8

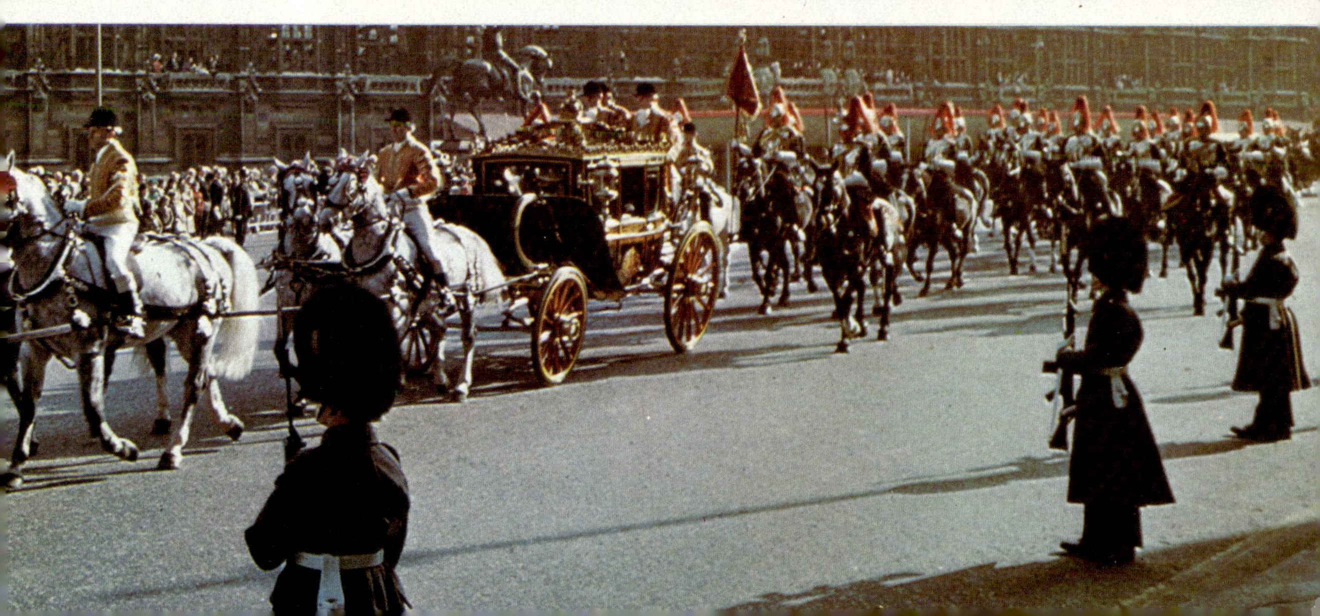

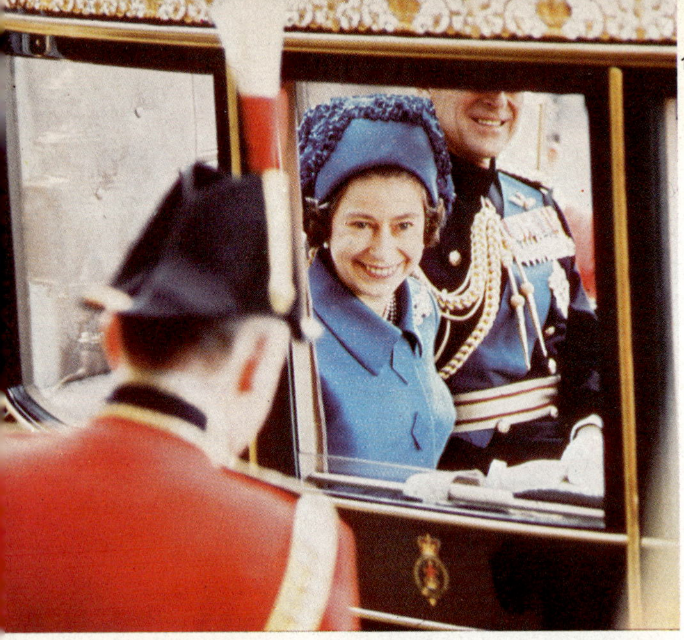

Westminster Abbey

Westminster Abbey, which is officially known as the Collegiate Church of St Peter in Westminster, is closely linked with the affairs of both Church and State and the Queen (shown here (10) arriving in her coach) attends the Abbey on many occasions. A Benedictine abbey, dedicated to St Peter, once stood on this site but it was rebuilt on a larger scale by Edward the Confessor and was consecrated in 1065. Of course, many additions have been made since then, the most important being the erection of the two west towers (12) during the eighteenth century. The interior of the Abbey contains many treasures, including the High Altar, before which monarchs are crowned, the Coronation Chair, dating from 1300, and the Stone of Scone, on which Scottish kings were crowned until it was captured in 1297 by Edward I. The greatest of England's poets are buried in Poets' Corner in the South Transept but the most famous grave here is that of the Unknown Warrior. This is an inscribed slab of black marble, surrounded by poppies, covering the body of a nameless representative of all our soldiers killed in the First World War. Wreaths are placed here at an annual service. Other services held in the Abbey include a Thanksgiving Service on Battle of Britain Day and a service at the Opening of the Law Courts. The most interesting custom here is the distribution of the Royal Maundy Money, which takes place every other year on Maundy Thursday. At this ceremony, which dates back to the Middle Ages when the sovereign gave alms to the poor, the Queen distributes specially minted silver coins to some of her subjects. On 28 December each year, (the anniversary of the Abbey's consecration) the Feast of the Holy Innocents is celebrated (11). For this occasion, plate and vestments that are usually hidden from the public gaze are displayed in all their glory. The Abbey is the last resting place of many of our sovereigns, including Edward the Confessor, its founder. William I was crowned here in 1066 and every monarch since then has also been crowned in Westminster Abbey. However, the greatest ceremony that the Abbey has seen in recent years was the marriage of Princess Anne to Captain Mark Phillips in 1973 (13). The Abbey, ablaze with colour, was packed to capacity, while those who were not invited thronged the streets to cheer the newly-weds or watched the service on television. Through the modern medium of broadcasting, millions of people all over the world are thus able to share some of the atmosphere and colour of the many pageants and ceremonies, traditional and contemporary, that are so intrinsic a part of the character of London.

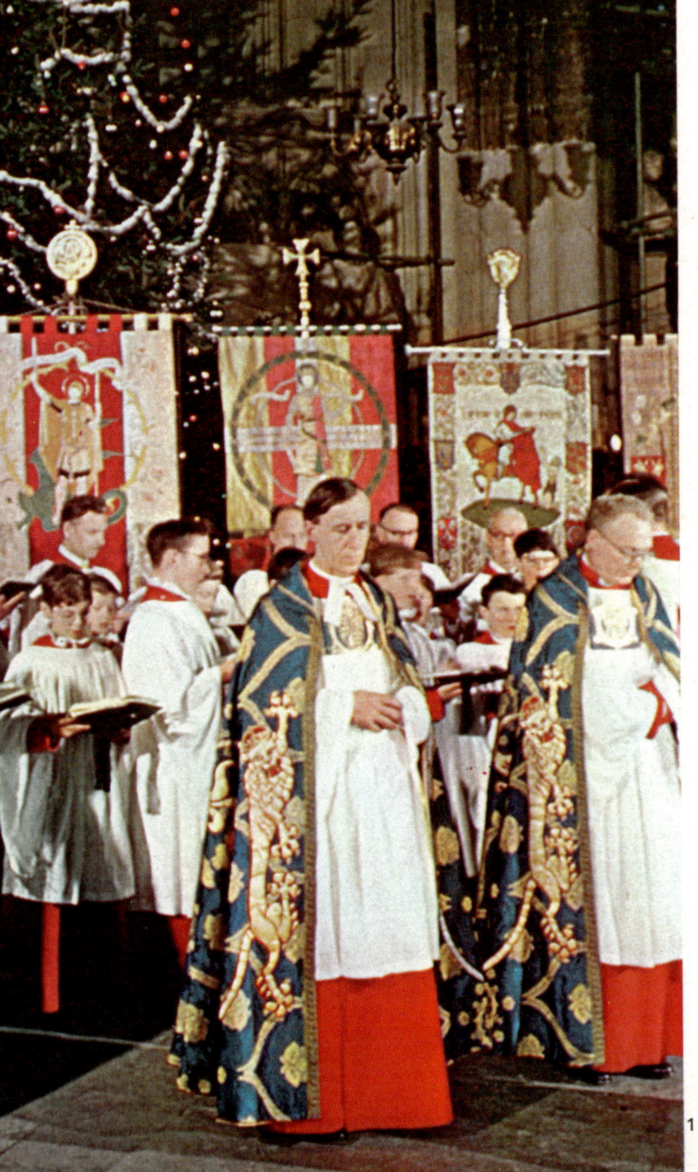

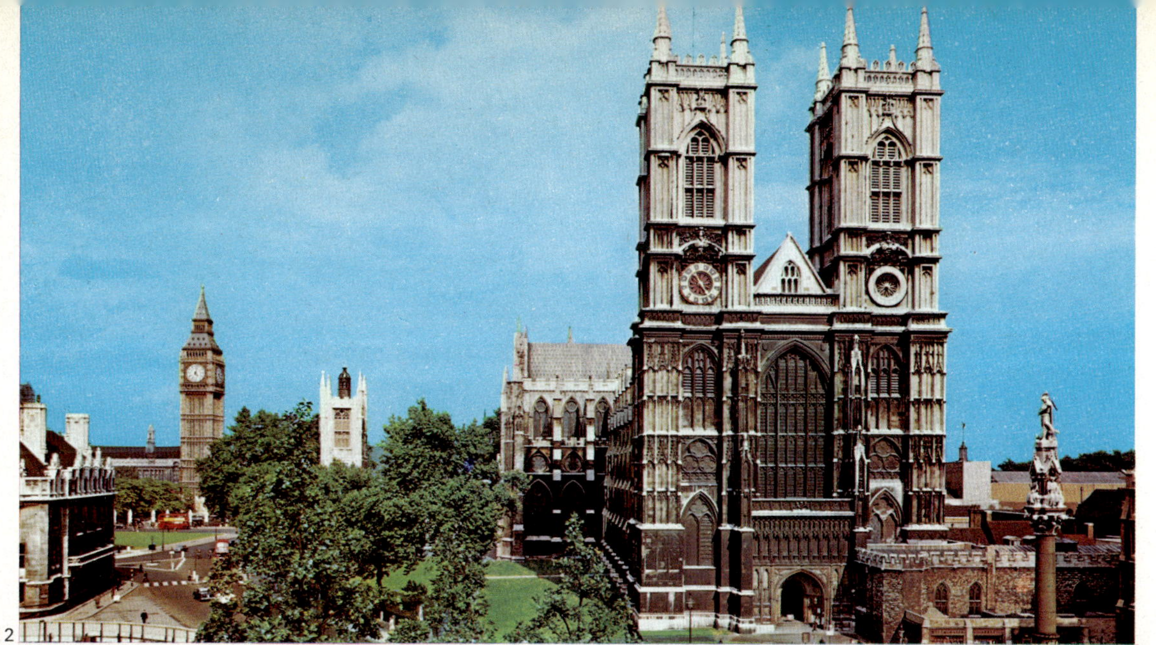

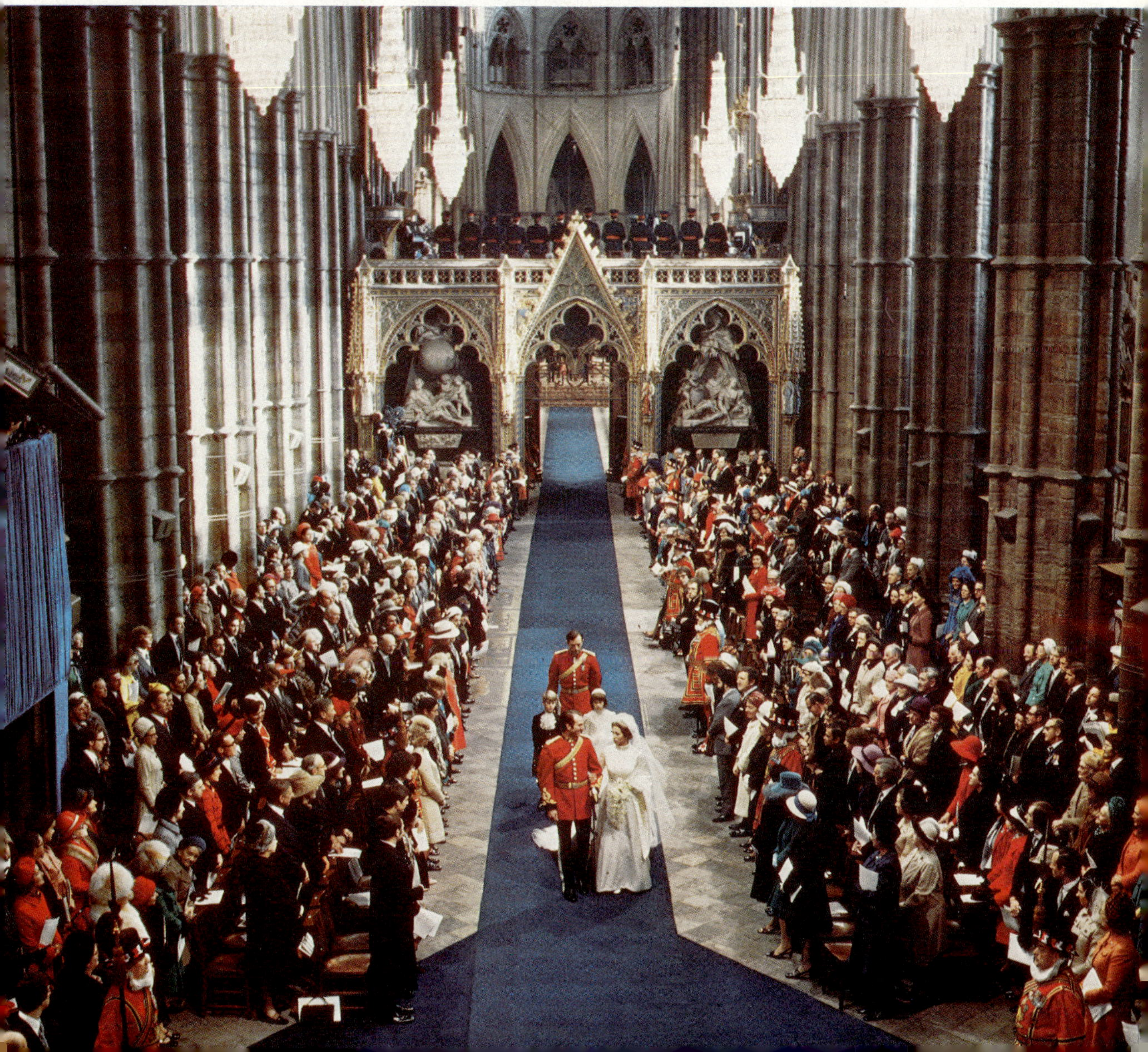

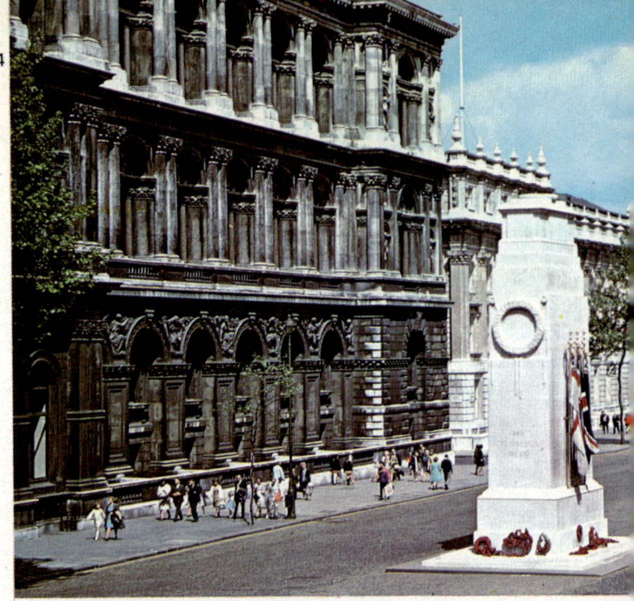

Whitehall

Whitehall is a great thoroughfare named after the Palace of Whitehall which was situated here until it was almost completely destroyed by a fire in 1698. All that remains of it today is the Banqueting Hall, from a window of which Charles I stepped to his execution in 1649. Whitehall is flanked by government buildings such as the War Office, the Foreign Office, the Admiralty Building, the Ministry of Agriculture and Fisheries and the Treasury, for this street is now the centre of England's modern bureaucratic administration. Conveniently situated nearby is No. 10 Downing Street, the official home of the Prime Minister of England. In the centre of Whitehall stands the Cenotaph (14), a plain white memorial to our dead of both the world wars, which was designed by Sir Edwin Lutyens. At first, this was intended to be a purely temporary structure, built for the Peace Celebrations in 1919 but, due to public demand, it was later re-erected as a more permanent monument. Every year since then, at 11 a.m. on Armistice Day, wreaths are laid around its base in a moving ceremony which is attended by the Queen and the Royal Family, the Prime Minister and many other delegates. A two-minute silence is observed at this service and, during this short space of time, the whole of London remains quiet in memory of its fallen heroes. On the west side of Whitehall stands Horse Guards, an eighteenth-century building with an imposing archway and a clock-tower, which was built on the site of the Guard House of the old Palace of Whitehall. Horse Guards, now the headquarters of the Home Forces, is always guarded by two dismounted sentries and two mounted Life Guards (1) or Royal Horse Guards. These are relieved every one or two hours, and the daily ceremony of the Changing of the Mounted Guard is held in the courtyard here (15). The Old Guard are relieved by the New Guard of twelve men, who are marched to Horse Guards from the Knightsbridge Barracks along the Mall. If the Queen is in residence in London, the New Guard is also accompanied by an Officer, a Standard-Bearer and the Queen's Trumpeter. The Royal Horse Guards and the Life Guards make up the two units of the Household Cavalry, whose main function during peace-time is to provide an escort for the Queen and for other important persons. The two regiments can be easily identified from their distinctive and colourful uniforms for, although they both wear cuirasses (breast and back plates), the Royal Horse Guards (16) have dark blue tunics and red plumes on their helmets, while members of the Life Guards (17) wear dashing red tunics and their helmets are topped by a white plume.

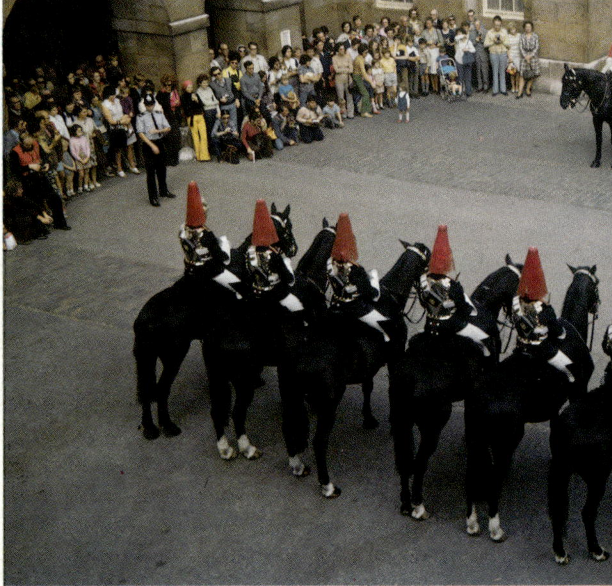

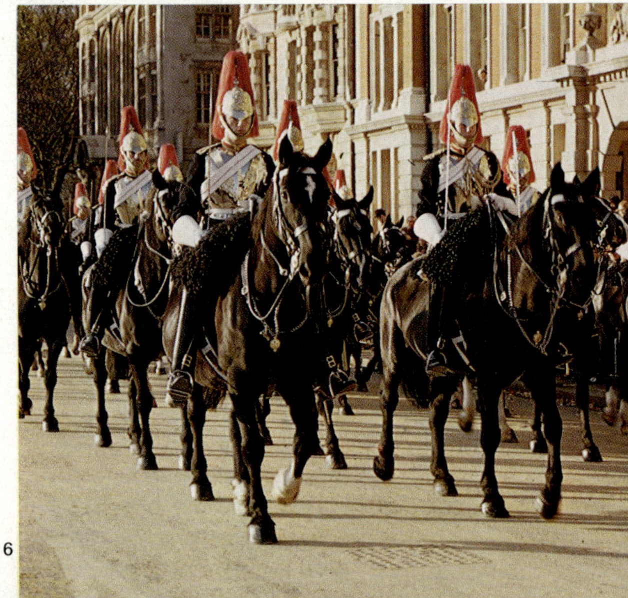

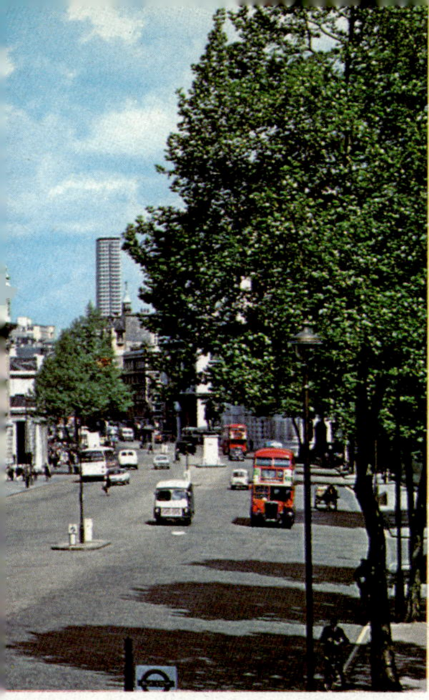

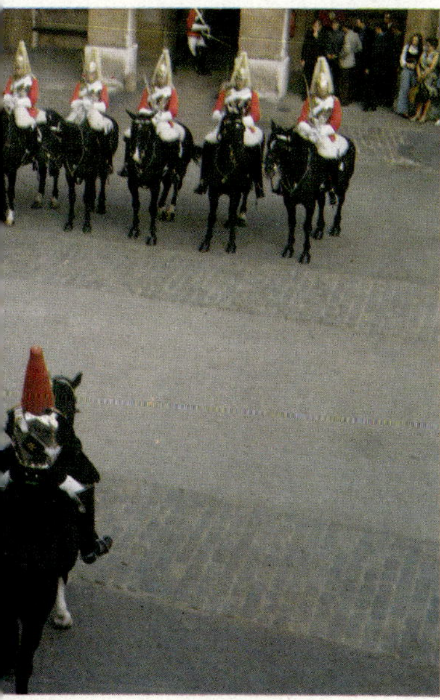

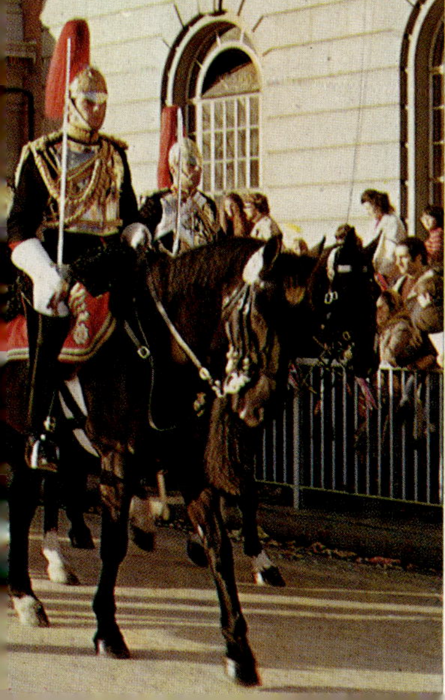

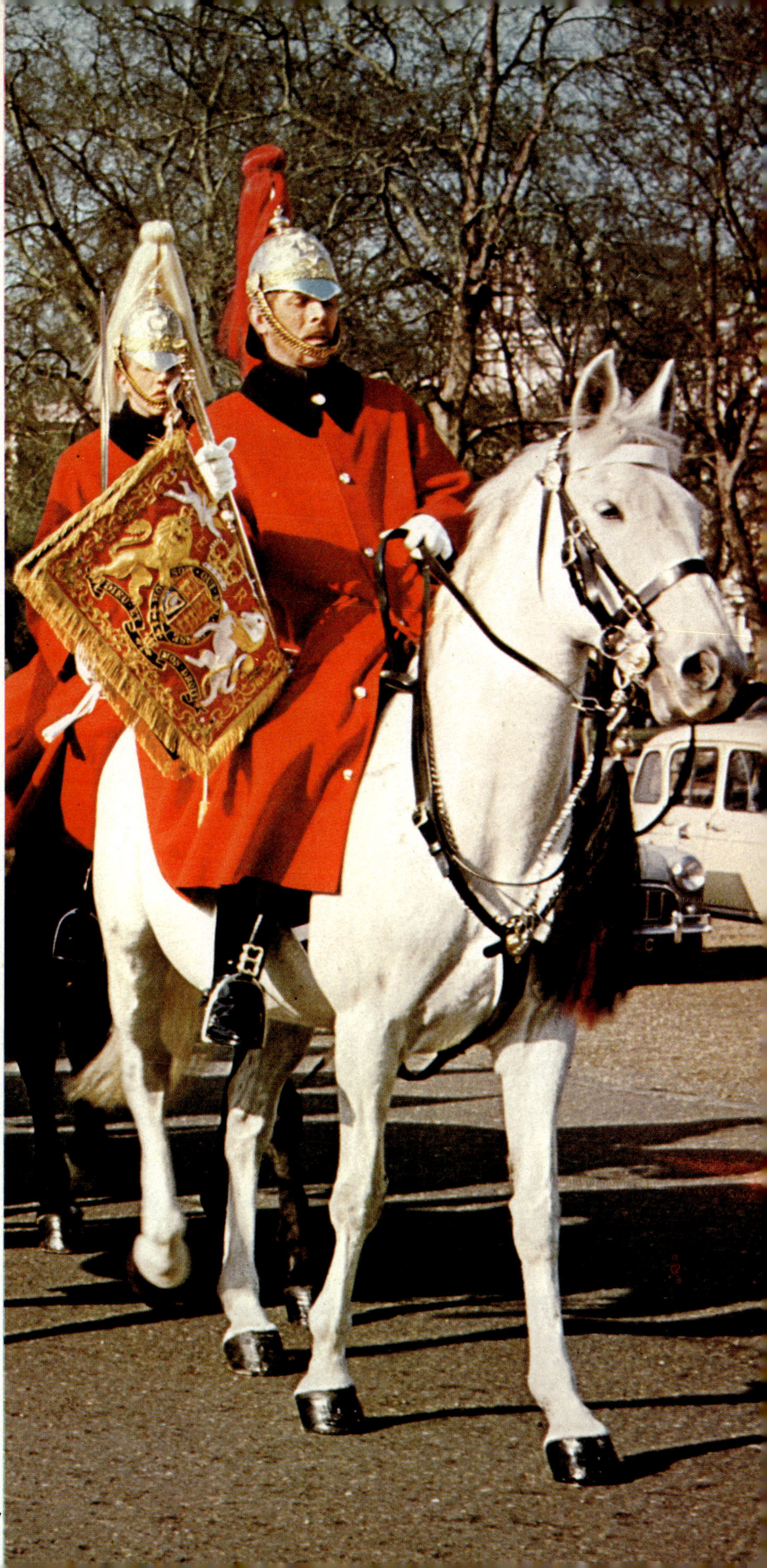

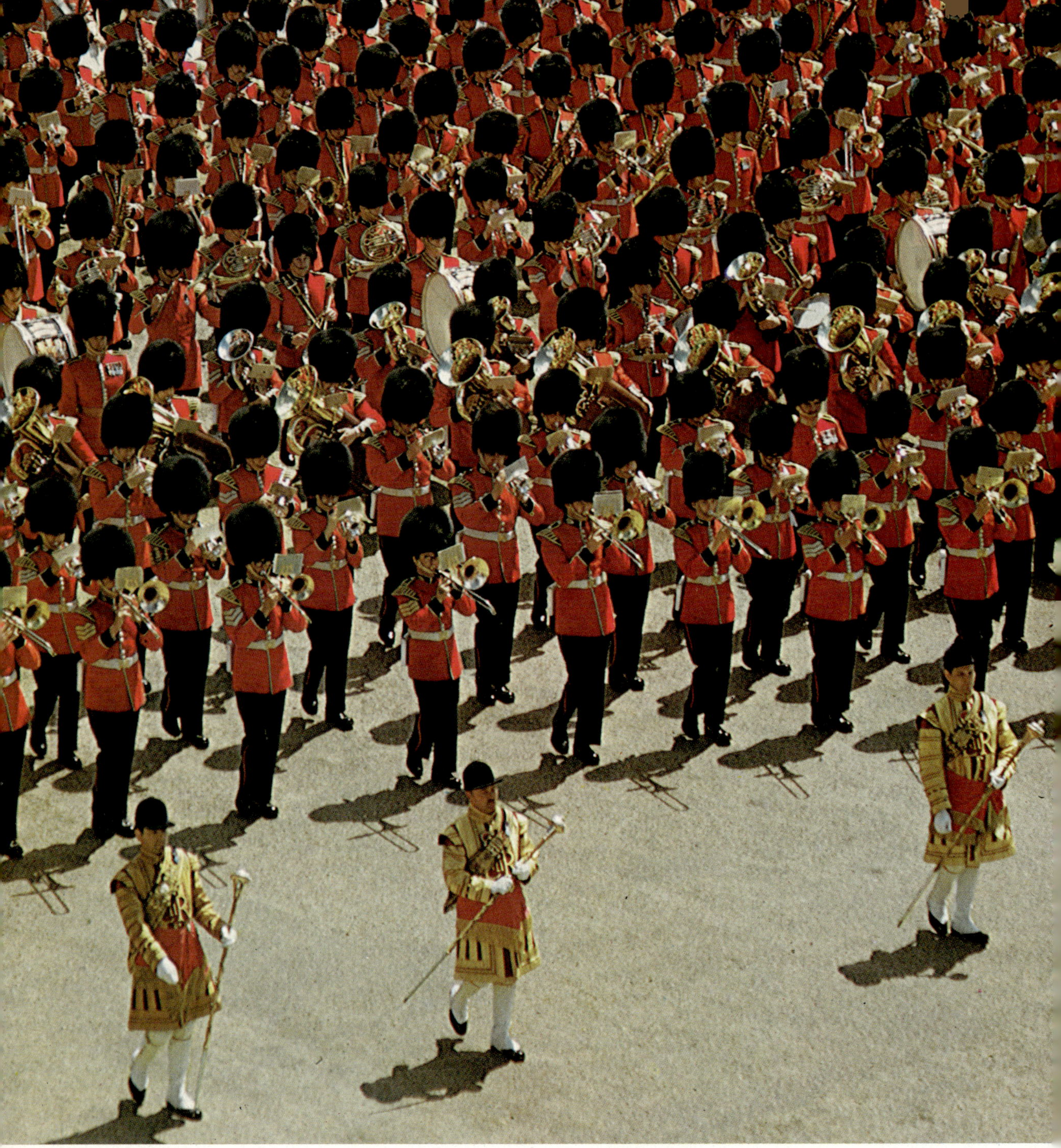

The Horse Guards Parade is a vast gravelled area bordering St James's Park, and it is here that one of London's most splendid pageants, Trooping the Colour, takes place in June each year. This military parade is held in honour of the Queen's Official Birthday and here (19), Her Majesty is shown crossing the Parade Ground to the saluting base. Visitors flock in their thousands to this event, yet few of them realise that Trooping the Colour (or flag) has its origins in earlier centuries when the regimental flag was used as a rallying point for troops in battle. Taking part in the display are the Household Cavalry, massed bands (18) and the five regiments which make up the Foot Guards. The Queen inspects this parade, then the Colour is trooped before her by the Foot Guards and dipped in salute. However, the climax of the ceremony is this combined march-past (20) in slow and then quick time, which calls for absolute precision, achieved through long periods of rehearsal.

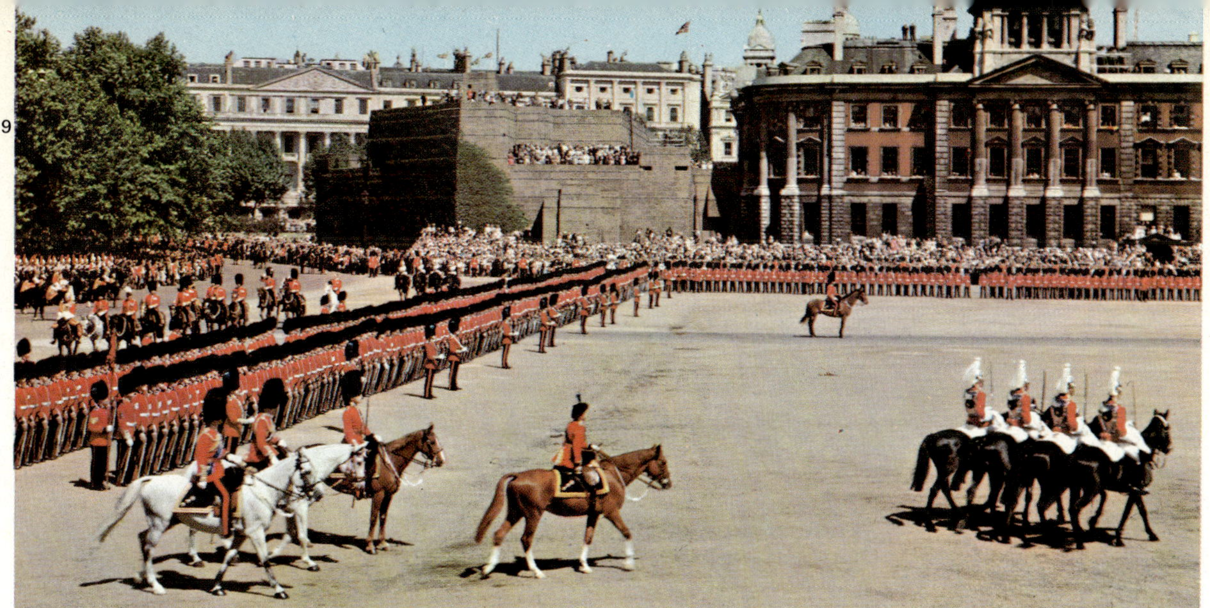

Despite the fact that Trooping the Colour only takes place once a year, there is always something of interest for the visitor to look at in the Horse Guards Parade. This is the largest clear space in London and so it is sometimes used as an emergency car park nowadays, yet no one can mistake its military associations. Statues which have been erected in the parade commemorate Field-Marshal Earl Kitchener of Khartoum, Field-Marshal Viscount Wolseley and Field-Marshal Lord Roberts, while on its west side, on the edge of St James's Park, is the Guards Division Memorial which commemorates the thousands of Guards who were killed during the First World War.

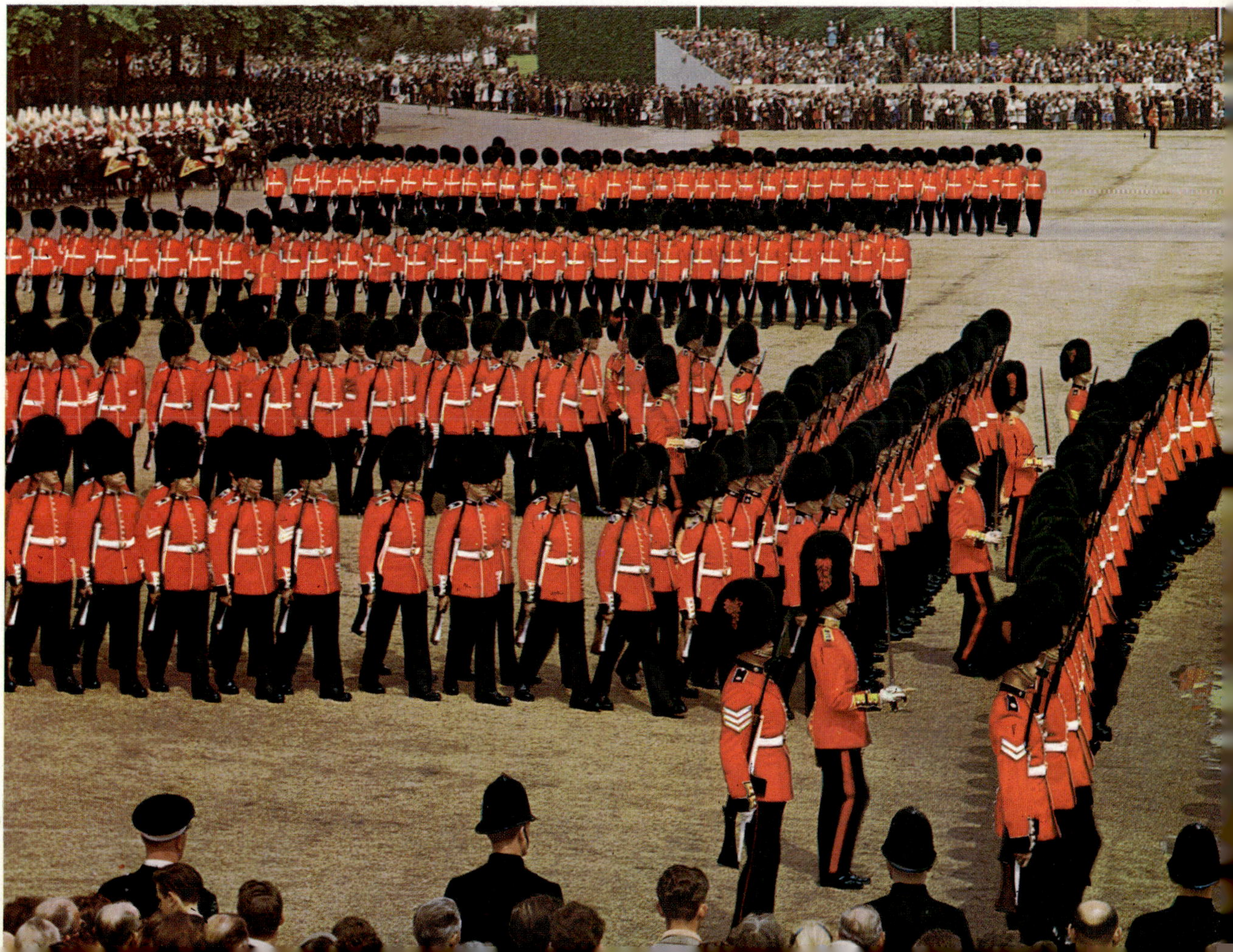

Buckingham Palace

Buckingham Palace (21) was named after Buckingham House, which was erected on this site by the Duke of Buckingham in 1705. George III then bought the house in 1762 and it was later remodelled by John Nash for George IV. Its dignified façade, one of London's greatest landmarks, was, in fact, only built in 1913 by Aston Webb. Since the accession of Queen Victoria in 1813, this palace has been used continuously as the official London residence of the Sovereign. The huge marble statue outside the Palace depicts Queen Victoria surrounded by figures of Justice, Truth and Motherhood, and surmounted by Courage, Constancy and the winged figure of Victory. Visitors can always find something of interest to watch, and these pictures show just a few of the many activities near the Palace. Here, for instance (22), a Band of Foot Guards marches down the Mall, which is a broad, tree-lined avenue leading to Buckingham Palace. A regimental trumpeter heads this parade of the Royal Horse Guards (23), while the Foot Guards, in this case (24) belonging to the Coldstreams, march precisely in step. One of the many attractions of Buckingham Palace are the military bands that can often be heard here, such as this band (25) of the Royal Artillery in the Mall, or the Guards' Band (26), shown leaving the Palace after Changing the Guard. The final picture (27) shows the trumpeters of the Household Cavalry.

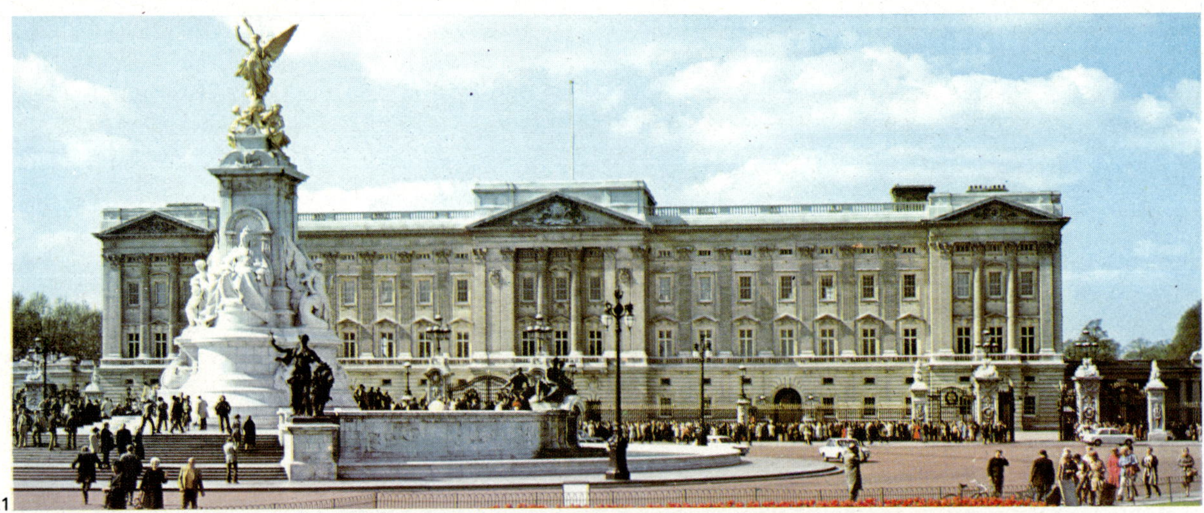

21

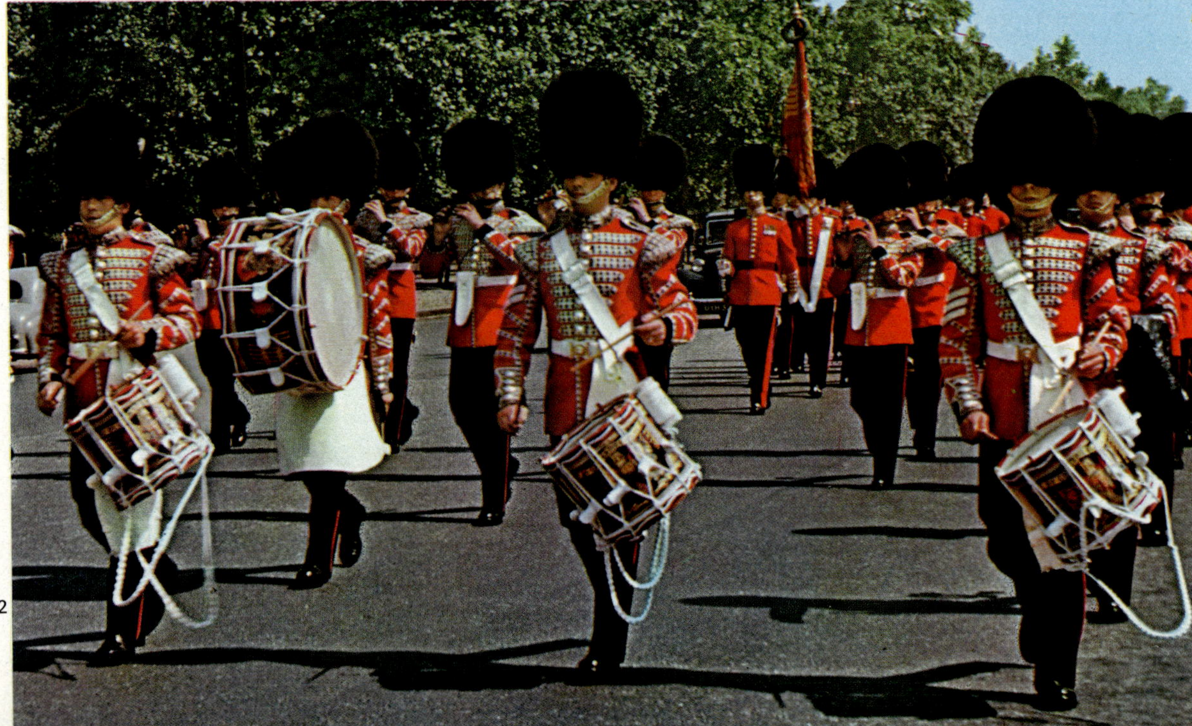

22

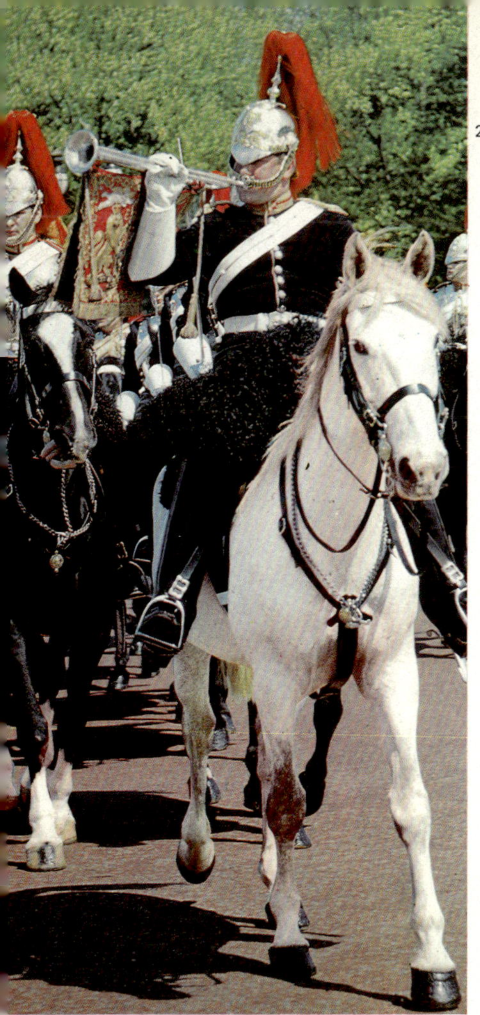

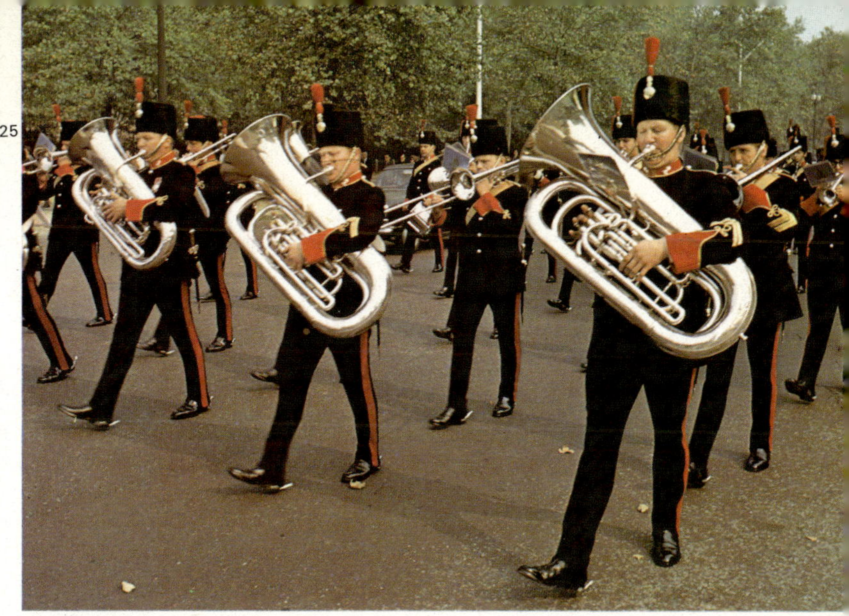

25

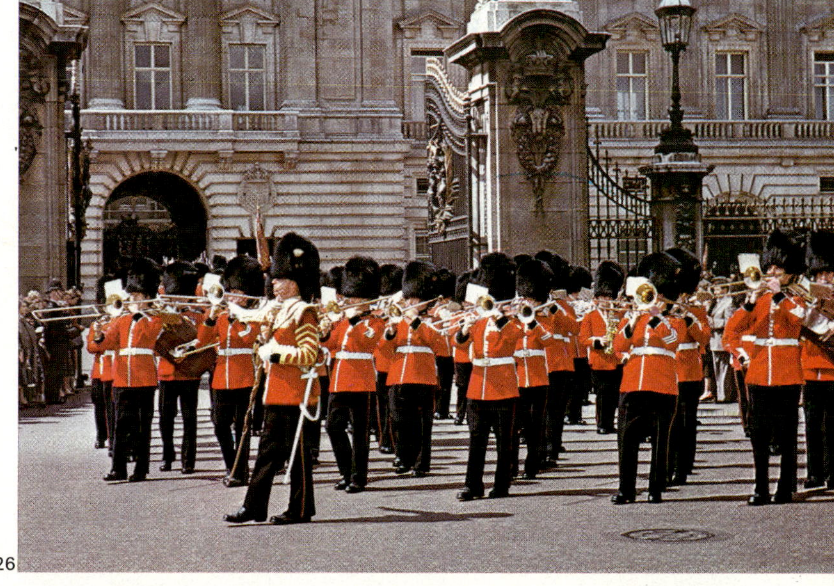

26

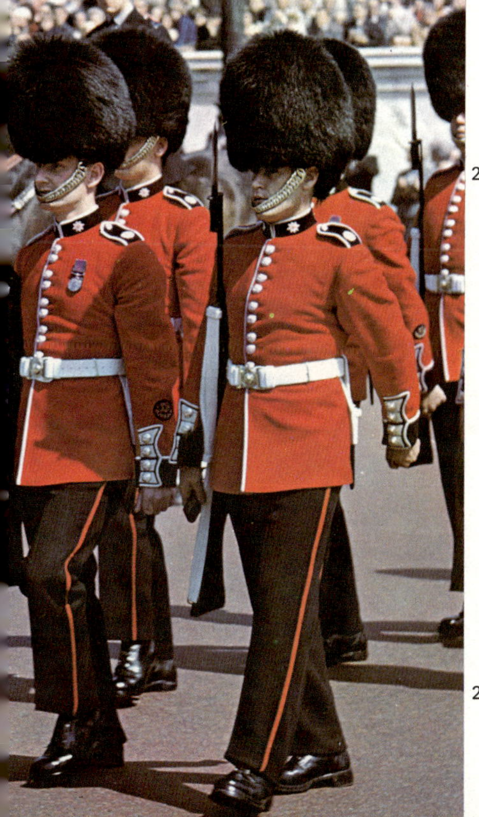

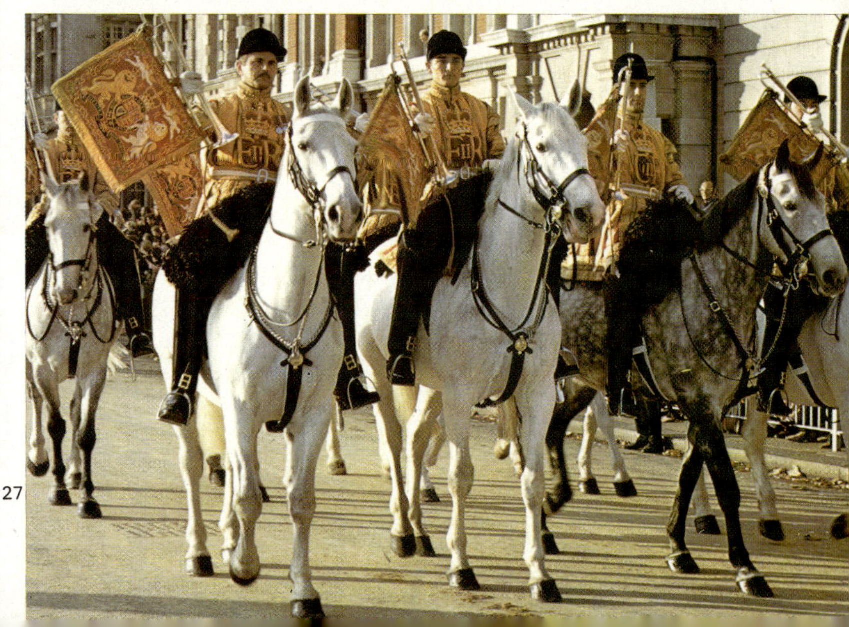

27

Her Royal Highness the Queen is only in residence at Buckingham Palace for a part of each year (the standard flying above the Palace signifies her presence), but even when the Royal Family is not there, the Palace is constantly protected by the Brigade of Guards, who take part in the ceremony of the Changing of the Guard each day. The Brigade of Guards is composed of the five units of Foot Guards: the Welsh Guards, the Irish Guards, the Scots Guards, the Coldstream Guards and the Grenadier Guards. These regiments are by no means just trained for ceremonial purposes for they were all originally formed as fighting units. The original Scots Guards, for instance, were completely wiped out in the Battle of Worcester in 1651, and the Grenadier Guards, so named because their main duty was to hurl the grenades in battle, were formerly attached to the Infantry of the British Army. Many of these Foot Guard regiments took part in active service in both the First and Second World Wars and, indeed, it was a bugler of the Scots Guards who sounded the Cease Fire in Europe in 1945. The Brigade of Guards all wear instantly recognisable uniforms of scarlet tunics and tall bearskins and, except to the observer who knows what to look for, it is hard to tell to which of the regiments they belong. In fact, each can be identified by the colour of the cockades in their bearskins and by the spacing of their tunic buttons. This photograph (28) shows one Guard from each of the five units, and they are, from left to right: the Coldstream Guards, with double-spaced buttons; the Irish Guards, with groups of four buttons; the Scots Guards, with groups of three buttons; the Welsh Guards, with groups of five buttons; and the Grenadier Guards, with single-spaced buttons. This pattern of buttons is also repeated on the cuffs of the tunic. The most famous ceremony at Buckingham Palace is, of course, the Changing of the Guard, which takes place daily at 11.30 a.m. unless the weather is particularly bad. First, the Queen's Colour is trooped from St James's Palace to Buckingham Palace and then the New Guard is led by a massed band from either the Chelsea or the Wellington Barracks. Once they have reached the Palace forecourt and taken their positions, they advance towards the Old Guard and touch hands in a gesture meant to symbolise the handing over of the keys. The Old Guard are then marched back to the barracks, again accompanied by the massed bands, and the New Guard are dismissed to take up their positions at the Palace, while a detachment of the New Guard march to St James's Palace to relieve the Old Guard there as well. Millions of visitors from all parts of the world come to watch this magnificent traditional ceremony, which lasts for about half an hour, and fortunately

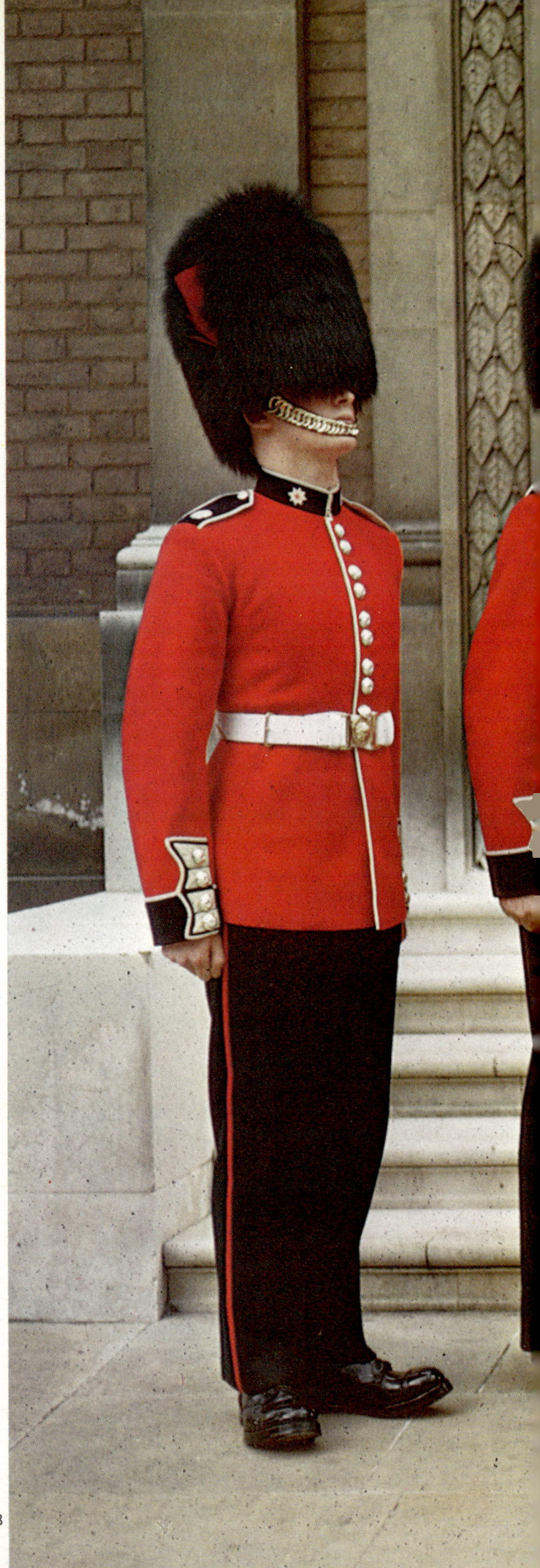

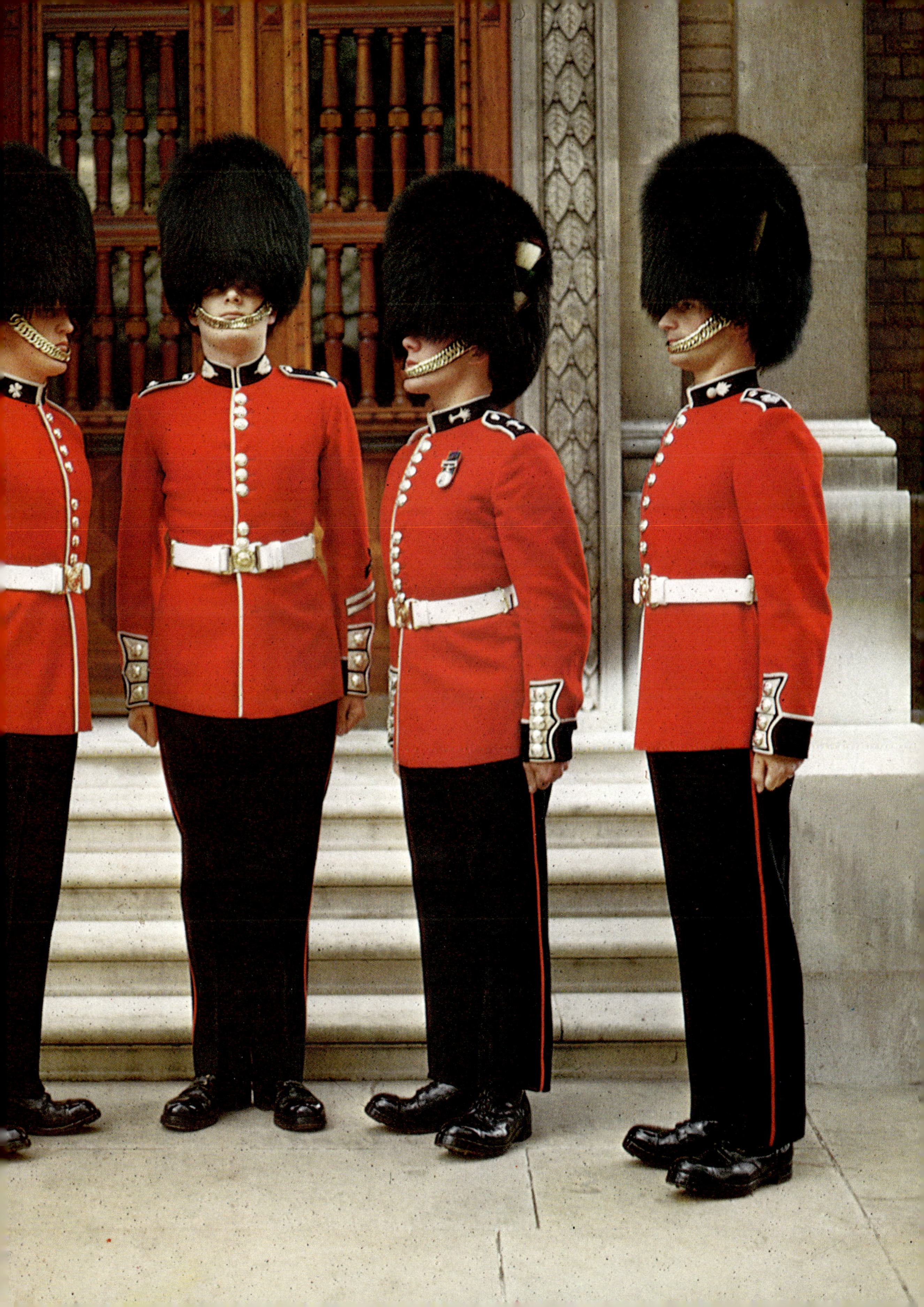

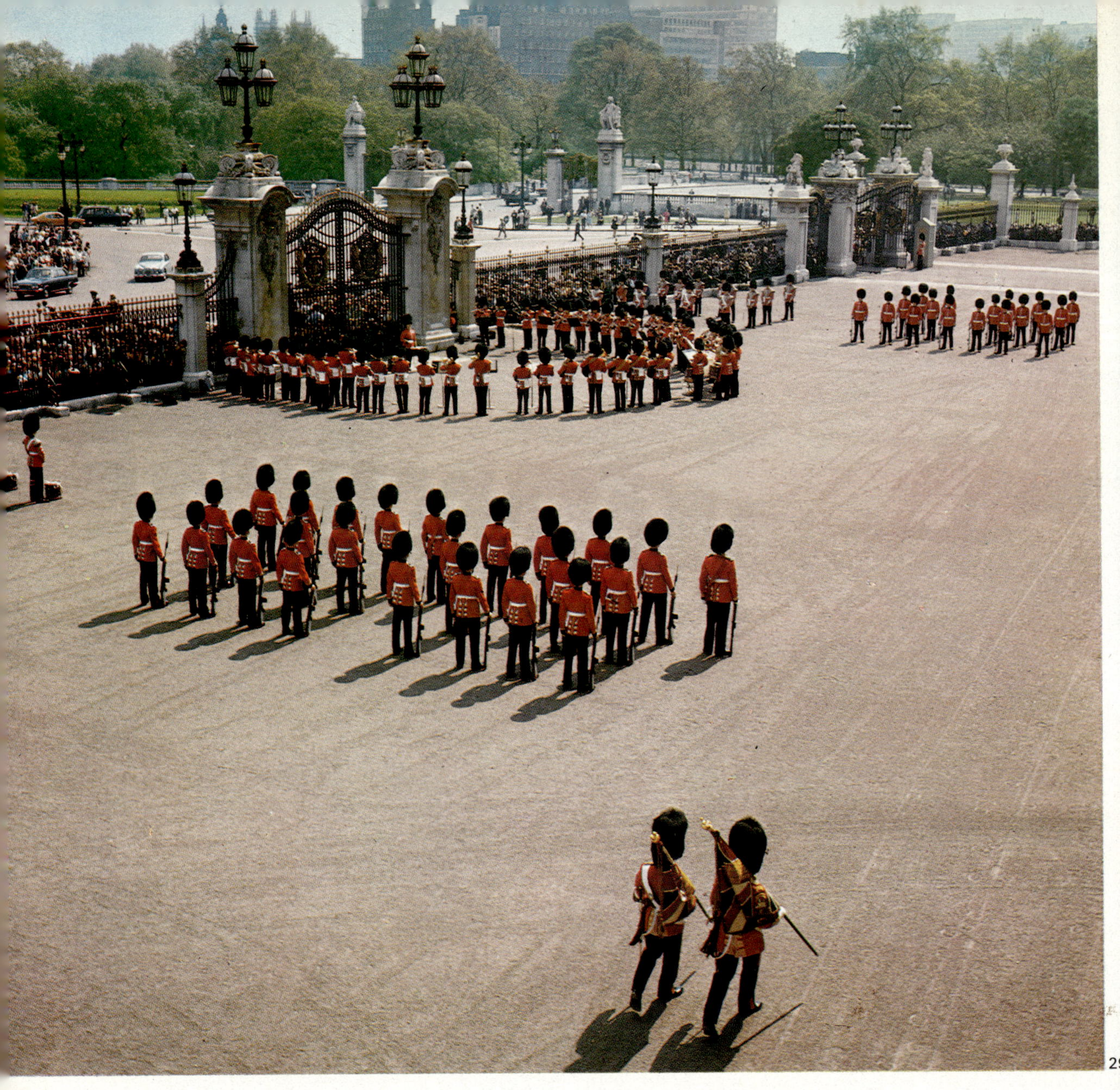

they can have an excellent view of the proceedings from behind the railings that surround the courtyard (29). When the Queen leaves Buckingham Palace on state occasions, she is always provided with a Royal Escort by the Household Cavalry, who are mounted on impeccably groomed horses that have been trained to disregard the noise of traffic and crowds. The Household Cavalry is composed of two regiments, the Royal Horse Guards and the Life Guards. The Royal Horse Guards, formed in 1661 from the remnants of Cromwell's new Model Army, were first commanded by the Earl of Oxford and this, combined with their dark blue uniform, earned them the soubriquet of the Oxford Blues, by which they are still known today. During the First World War they served as both cavalry and infantry and in the Second World War they were amalgamated with the Life Guards. The Life Guards (30) are the foremost regiment of the British Army, although they are not the oldest, and once membership of the Life Guards was considered such an honour that recruits actually had to pay to enlist. They were formed in 1660 as a bodyguard for Charles II and originally consisted of two troops, one known as the King's Troop while the other was the Duke of York's Troop. In 1922, the Life Guards were amalgamated with the Royal Horse Guards to become the Household Cavalry. The regiments were fully mechanised and it was only at the end of the Second World War, in 1945, that a squadron was again mounted and assigned to the ceremonial duties with which we always associate the Household Cavalry today.

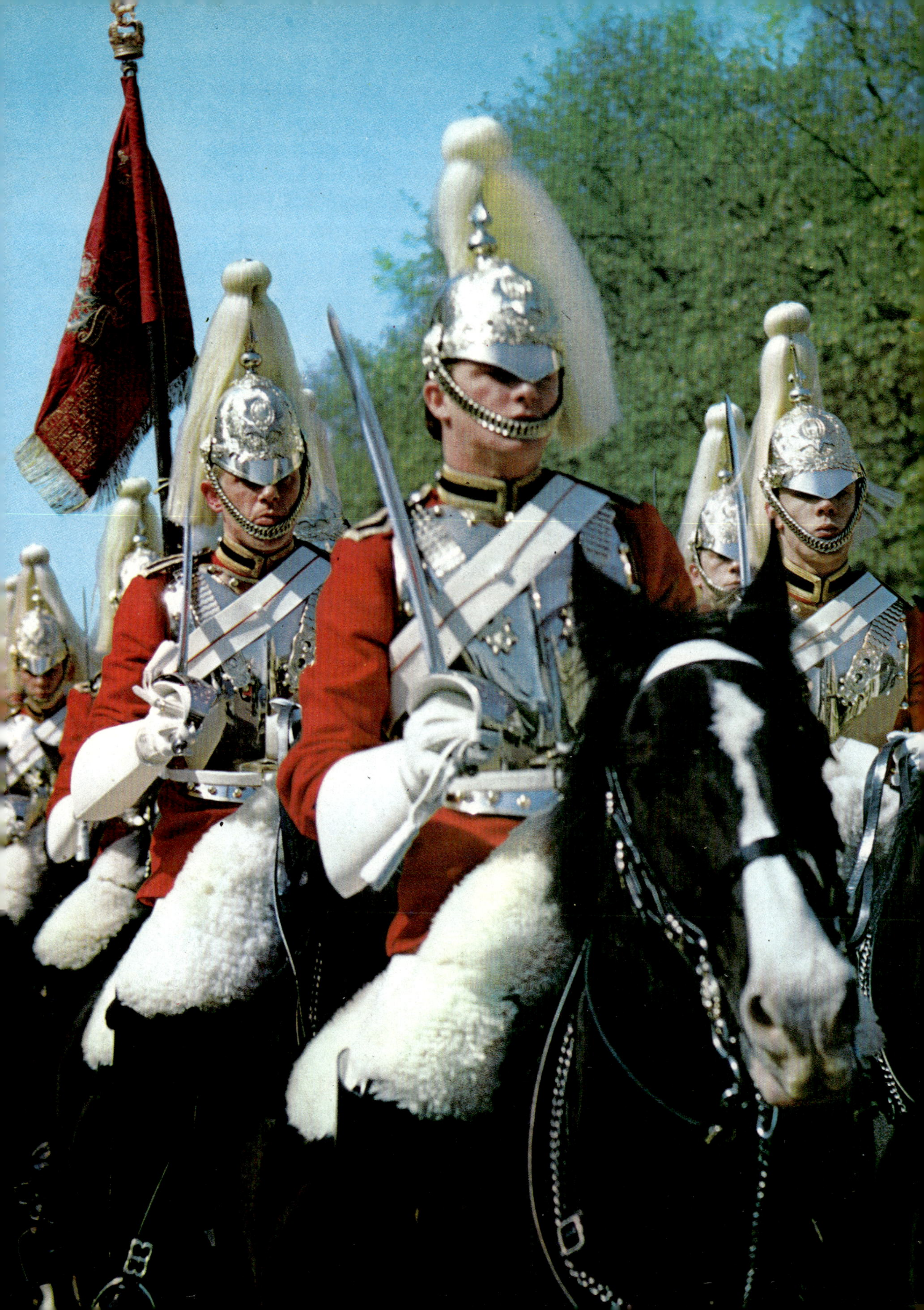

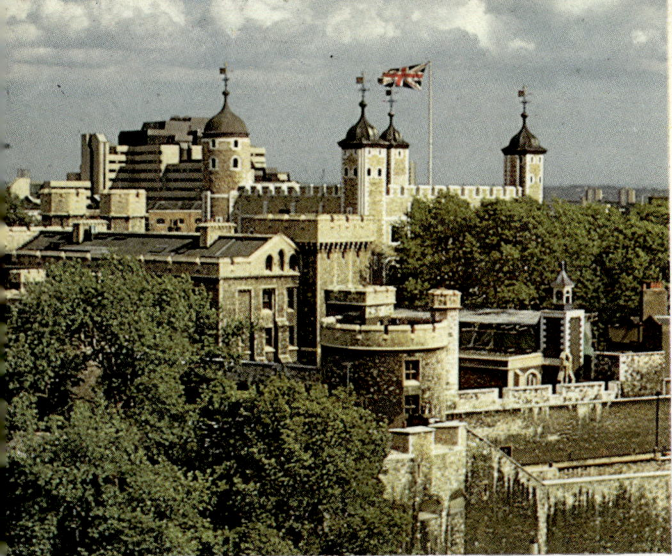

The Tower of London

The Tower of London (31) was founded in 1078 by William the Conqueror, who built the Keep, or White Tower, while the surrounding buildings were added over the centuries. Many atrocities were committed behind its walls, such as the cold-blooded murder of the two little Princes in the Bloody Tower and the executions of Anne Boleyn, Catherine Howard, Lady Jane Grey and Sir Thomas More but, as well as acting as a prison and fortress, it has also been a Garrison, a Wardrobe, a Menagerie and a Royal Palace, while today it is a Museum and houses the National Collection of Armour and the Crown Jewels. The Tower is always attended by a detachment of the Yeomen of the Guard, who were originally formed to be a bodyguard for Henry VII, after the Battle of Bosworth in 1485. Their duties included making the king's bed and guarding his buffet, and it is probably from this latter that they derived their familiar name 'Beefeaters' (from the Norman-French *boufitier*), though many other theories have been suggested. The Yeoman Warders still wear the Tudor uniform (32) chosen for them by the king though a ruff was added by Elizabeth I, while Queen Victoria introduced an 'undress' uniform for everyday use. On state occasions, the Chief Warder bears a mace, the Yeoman Gaoler carries the ceremonial axe and the others hold partisans, or pikes. On Ascension Day every third year, the Yeoman Warders take part in the old custom of Beating the Bounds (33). This custom, which entails boys (chosen from families who live in the Tower) beating the thirty-one Crown Boundary Marks with white willow wands, originated in the Middle Ages when maps were scarce, so the boundaries of each parish had to be individually pointed out every so often. The most famous custom at the Tower, however, is the Ceremony of the Keys (34), which takes place every night at 10 o'clock. The Chief Warder, shown here in full ceremonial dress (35), and his escort march to the outer gate of the Tower, lock it and then proceed to the gates of the Middle and Byward Towers, which are also locked. On their return journey, a sentry at the Bloody Tower challenges them thus — 'Halt! Who goes there?' The Chief Warder then replies, 'The Keys.' 'Whose Keys?' 'Queen Elizabeth's Keys', at which they are told 'Pass Queen Elizabeth's Keys. All is well.' The main guard wait on the steps beyond to present arms to the party. Here, the Chief Warder raises his Tudor bonnet and says 'God preserve Queen Elizabeth', to which all answer 'Amen' (36). The Last Post is then sounded and the Keys are delivered to the Resident Governor. From now on, nobody can enter the Tower without the password.

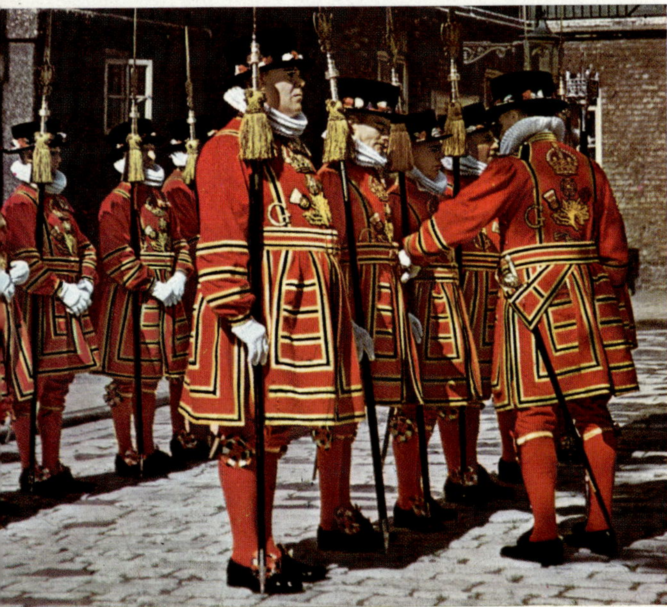

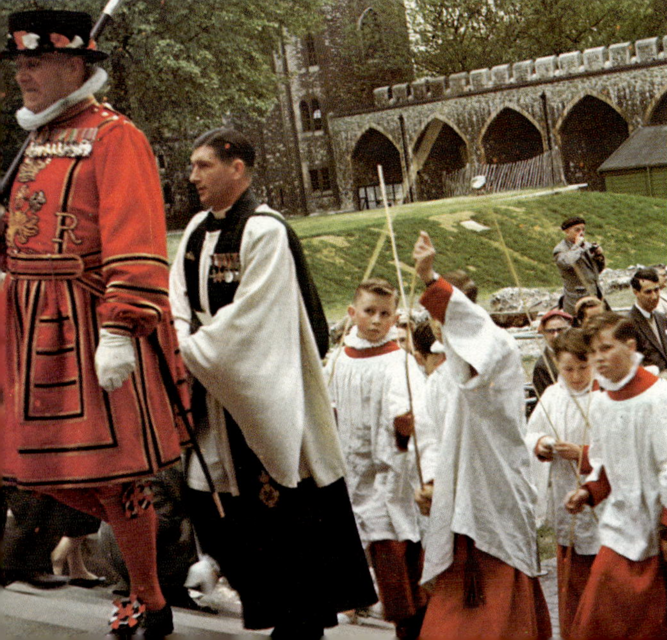

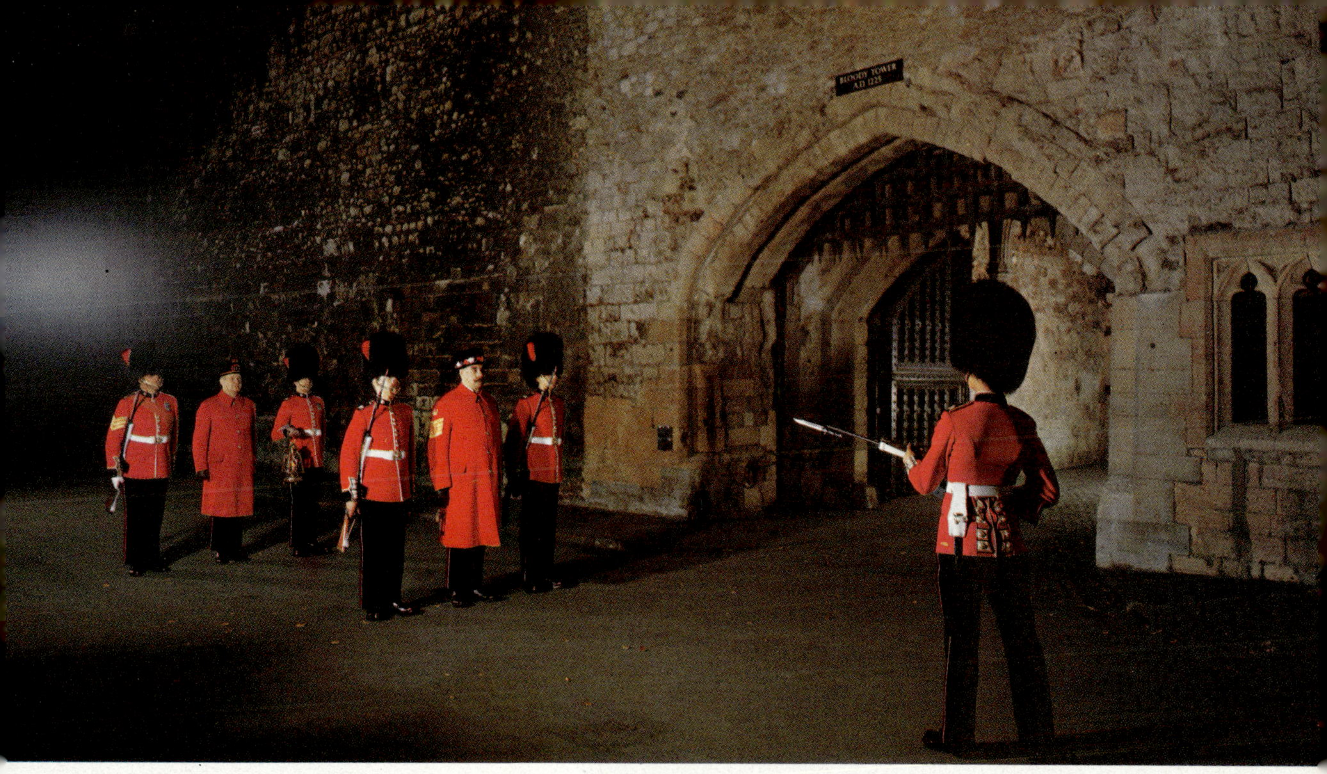

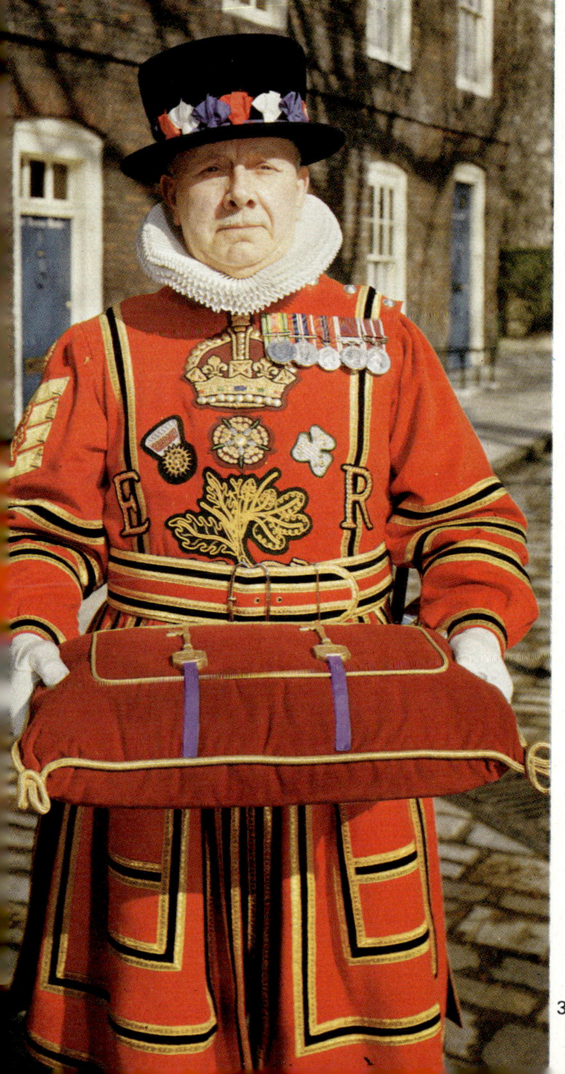

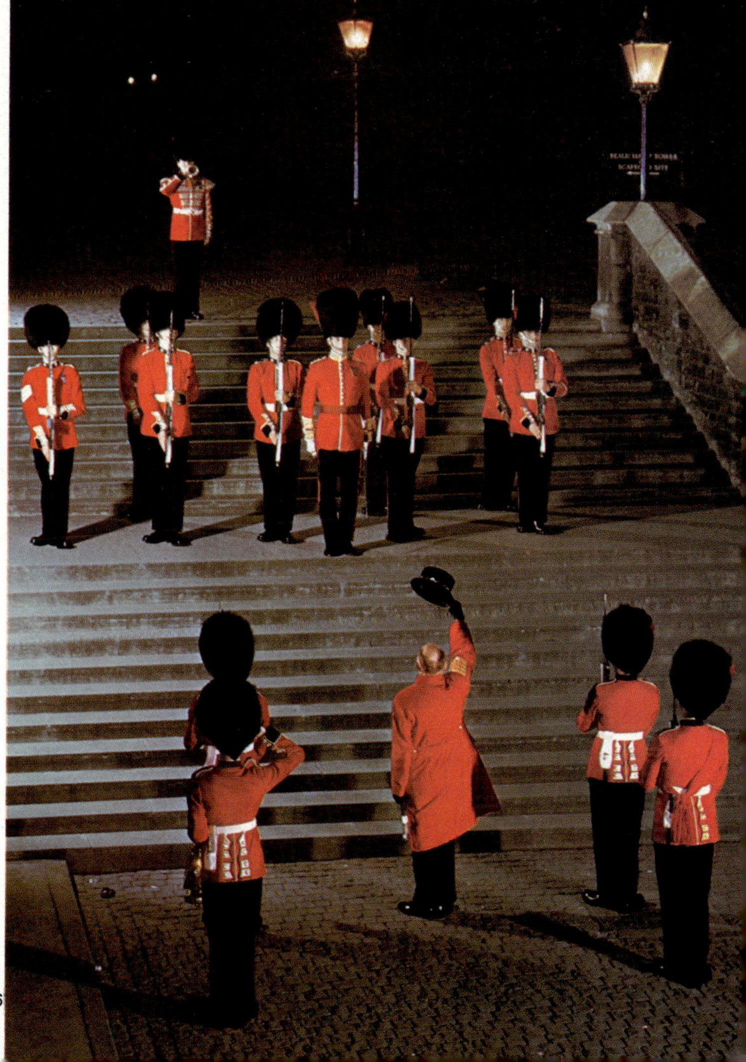

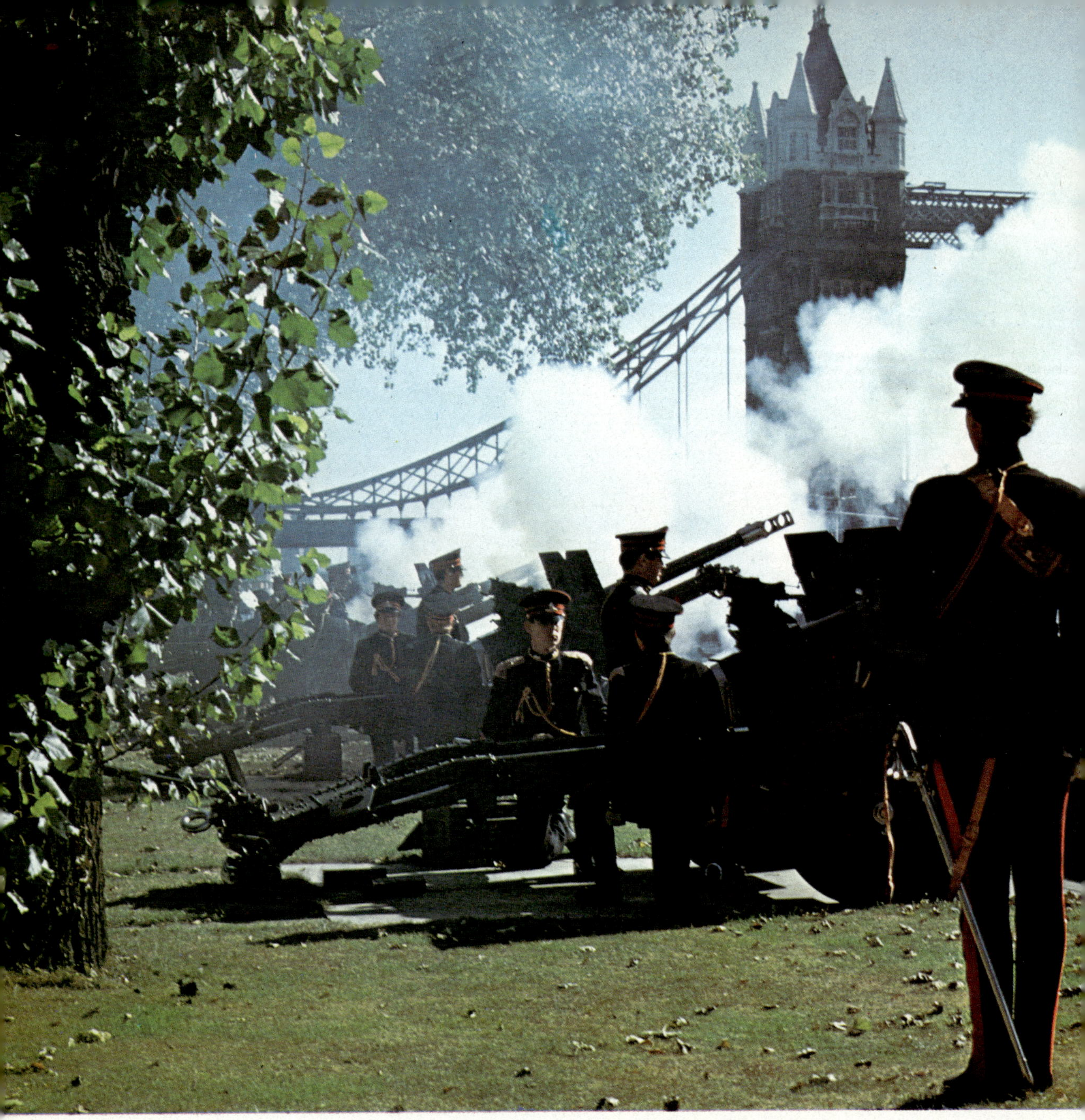

Situated on the bank of the Thames is the Wharf of the Tower of London. Here is a collection of guns including bronze Turkish, Chinese and Indian guns and some specimens from the Napoleonic and the Crimean Wars. At the west end of the Wharf is the Gun Park (37), where salutes are fired by the Honourable Artillery Company — sixty-two rounds are fired for royal anniversaries and forty-one on other occasions, such as the State Opening of Parliament. In the background of this photograph rise the two massive steel towers of Tower Bridge, faced with granite and Portland stone. The bridge was opened in 1894 and the precision engineering which raises its bascules (each of which weighs about 1,000 tons) in a matter of minutes to let ships pass through has never yet failed. Ravens, once used as scavengers, have lived in the Tower of London for centuries. Legend has it that, if the ravens leave, the British Empire will crumble and the Tower itself will fall, so the six that are kept here today (38) periodically have their wing-feathers clipped by the Raven-Master so that they cannot fly out of the environs of the Tower. The ravens can normally be seen strutting across Tower Green (though visitors should not venture too close as these birds can be vicious).

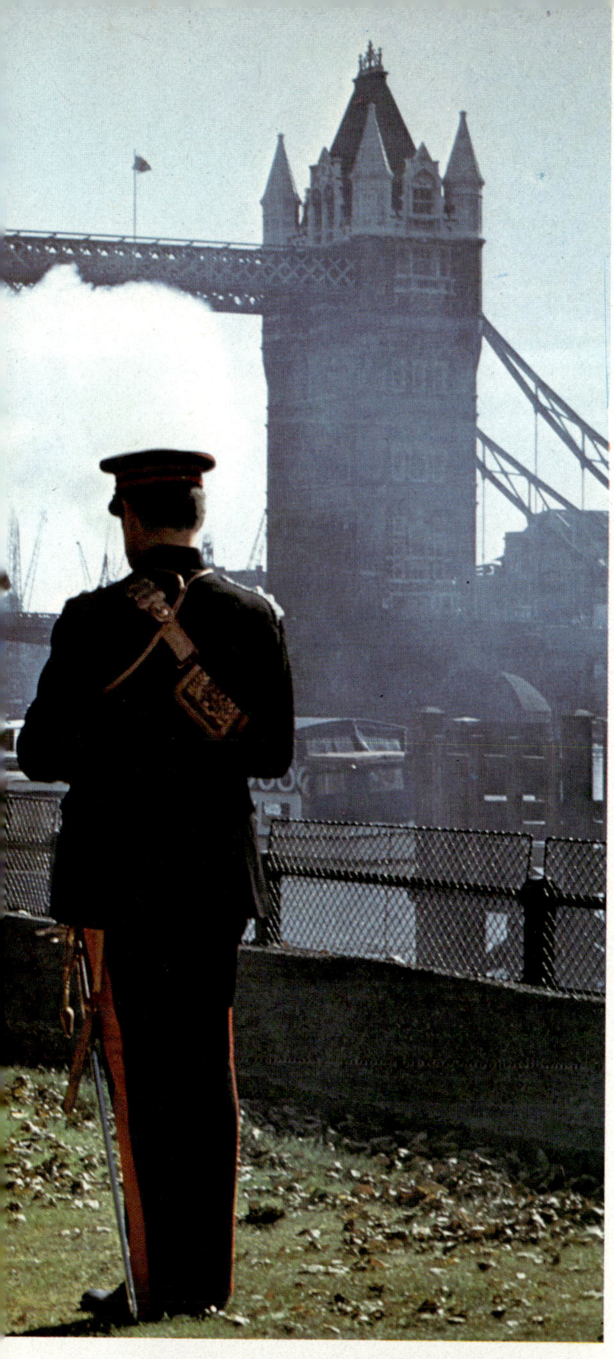

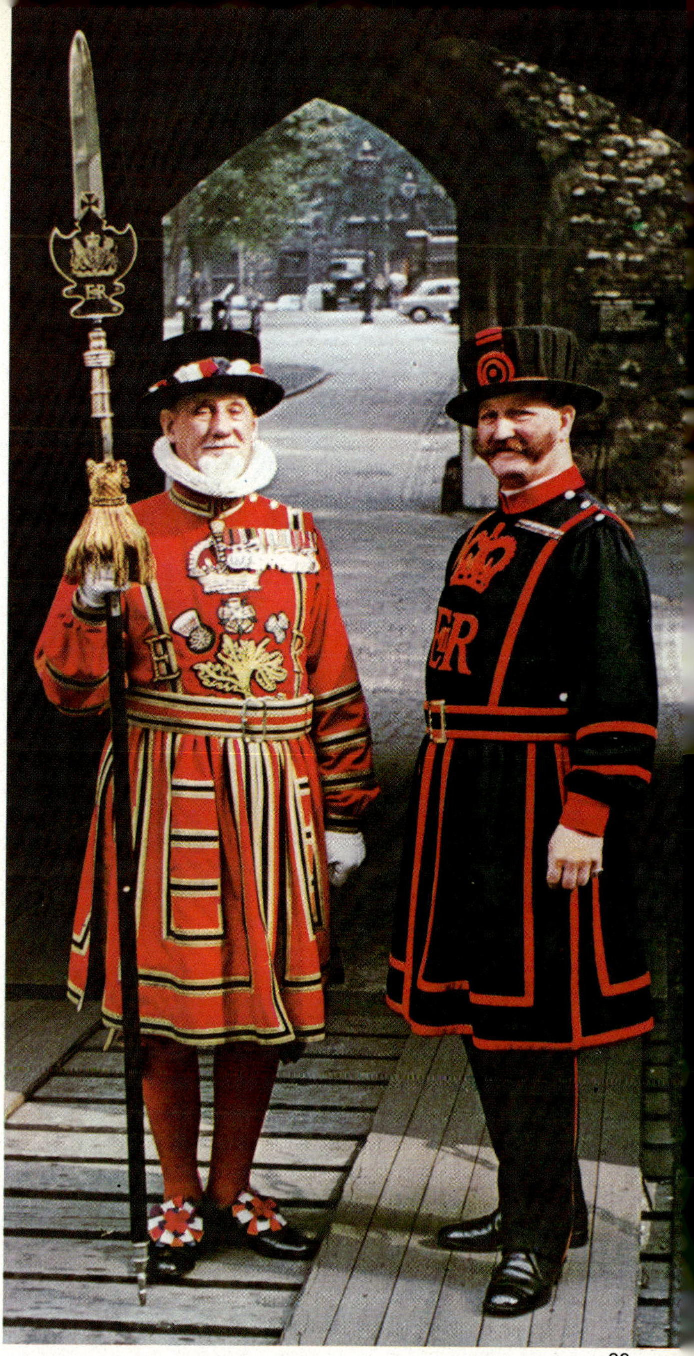

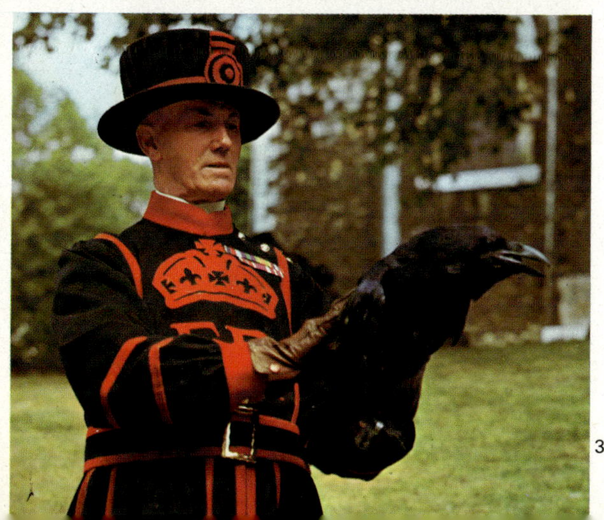

39

Once, anyone could become a Yeoman Warder by the simple expedient of paying £309 but, when the Duke of Wellington was made Constable of the Tower, he abolished this purchase of office and, nowadays, the Yeomen of the Guard (there are about forty of them at the Tower) are chosen from retired warrant and non-commissioned Army officers. This picture (39) shows the two uniforms that are worn by the Yeoman Warders. On the left is the state uniform chosen by Henry VII, resplendent in red and gold for ceremonial occasions, while on the right is the dark blue and red undress uniform, introduced by Queen Victoria in 1858 for everyday wear.

The Chelsea Pensioners

The Chelsea Royal Hospital was founded by Charles II in 1682 for veteran and disabled soldiers, and the building itself was built by Sir Christopher Wren. The Chelsea Flower Show is held each May in the spacious gardens. The Hospital still cares for retired soldiers, known affectionately as Chelsea Pensioners, in return for their wartime services to the country.

Every year on Oak Apple Day, which is the anniversary of the restoration of Charles II, their founder, a ceremony is held outside the Hospital (40). The Pensioners' colourful uniforms are adapted from those worn during the eighteenth century by the Duke of Marlborough's armies. In winter, the uniform consists of a dark blue overcoat but in summer the Pensioners wear distinctive scarlet frock coats (41) with a peaked cap or, for ceremonial wear, a three-cornered hat.

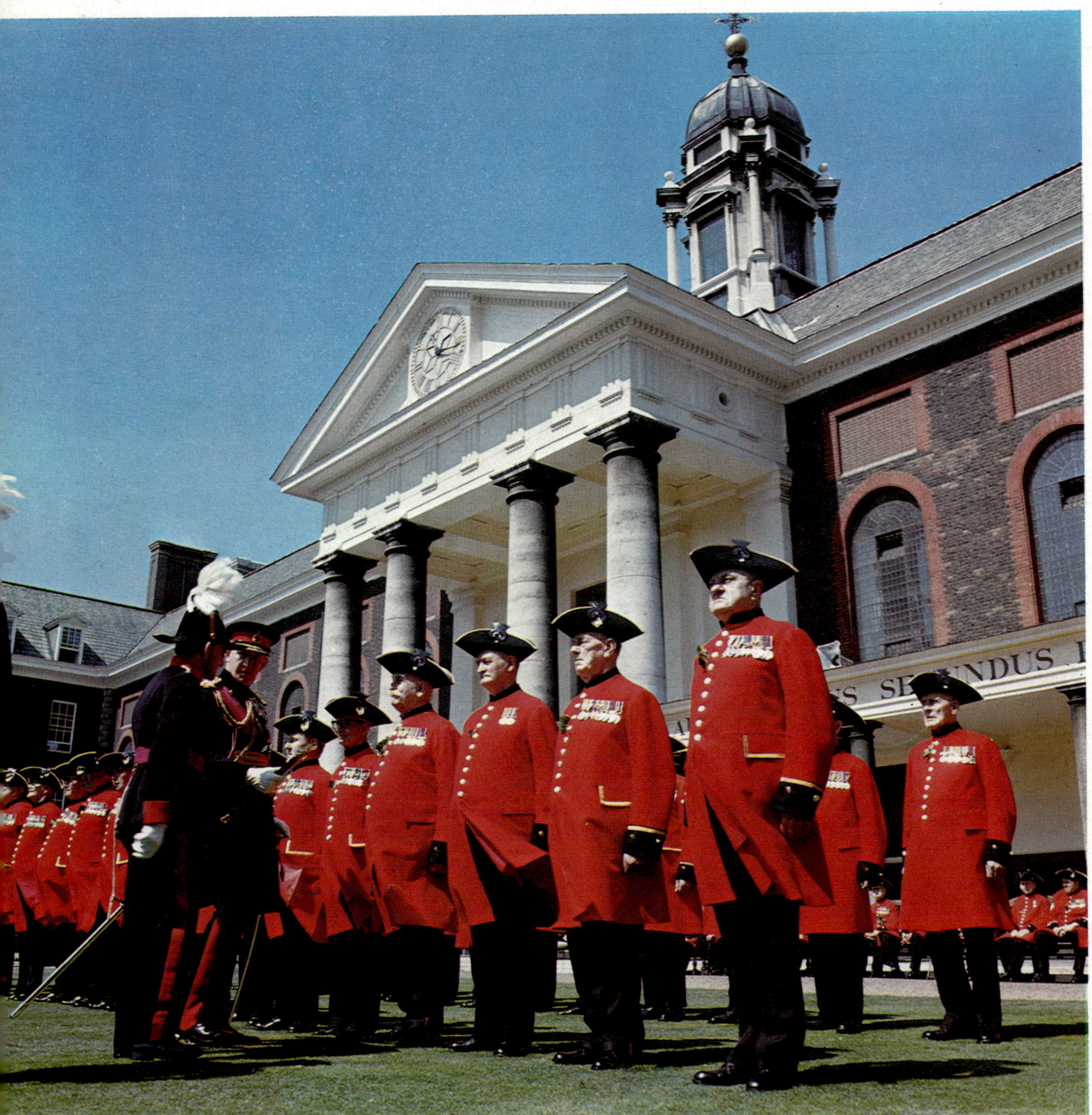

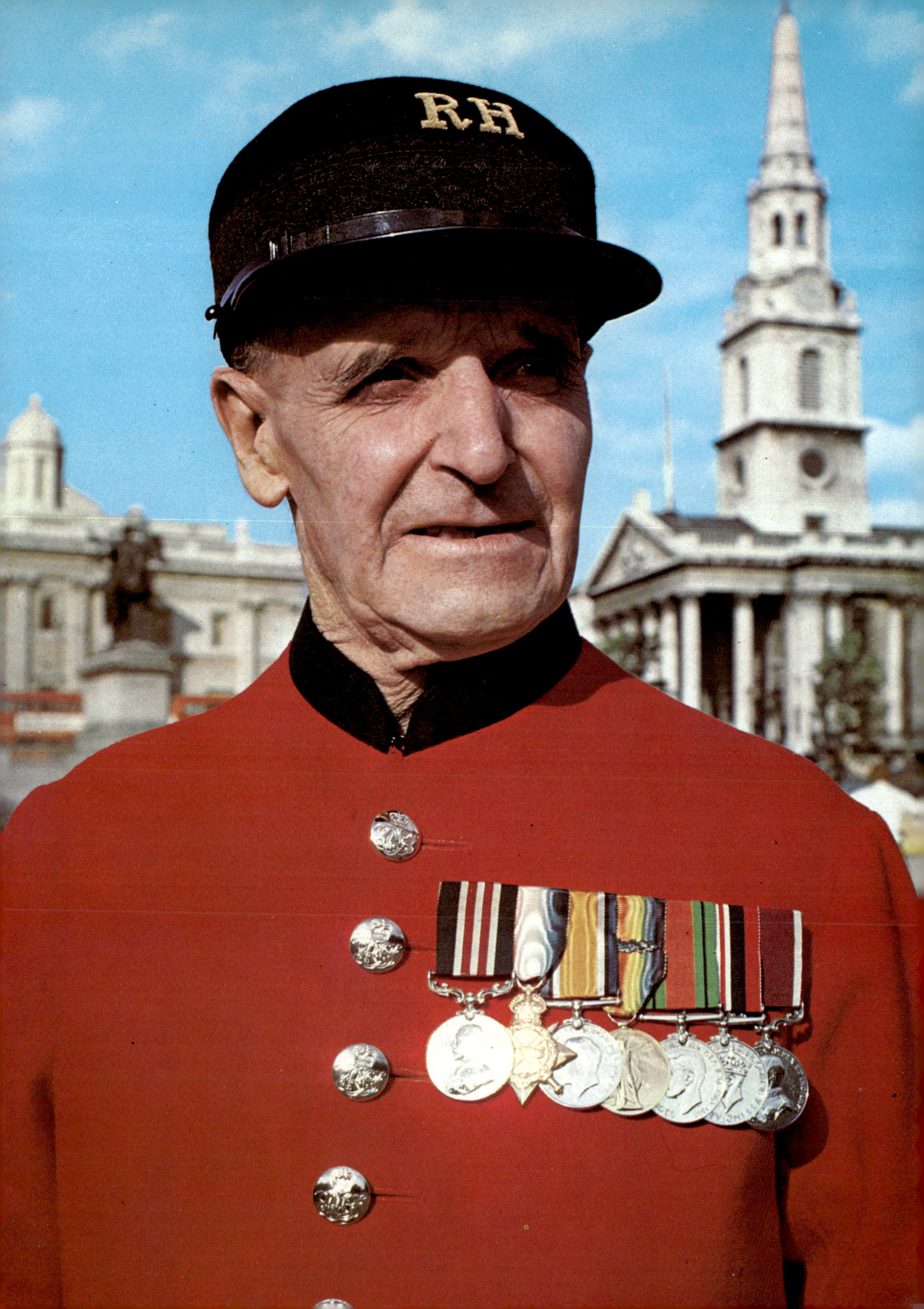

Despite London's overall impression of noise and congestion, it actually has more than 150 parks, where the busy outside world can be temporarily forgotten. Here, trees and grass act as a perfect backdrop for the colour of London's pageantry. These photographs show an Officer and Trumpeter of the Royal Horse Guards (42) and 'Cicero', the gaily decked drum horse of the Household Cavalry (43) in Hyde Park.

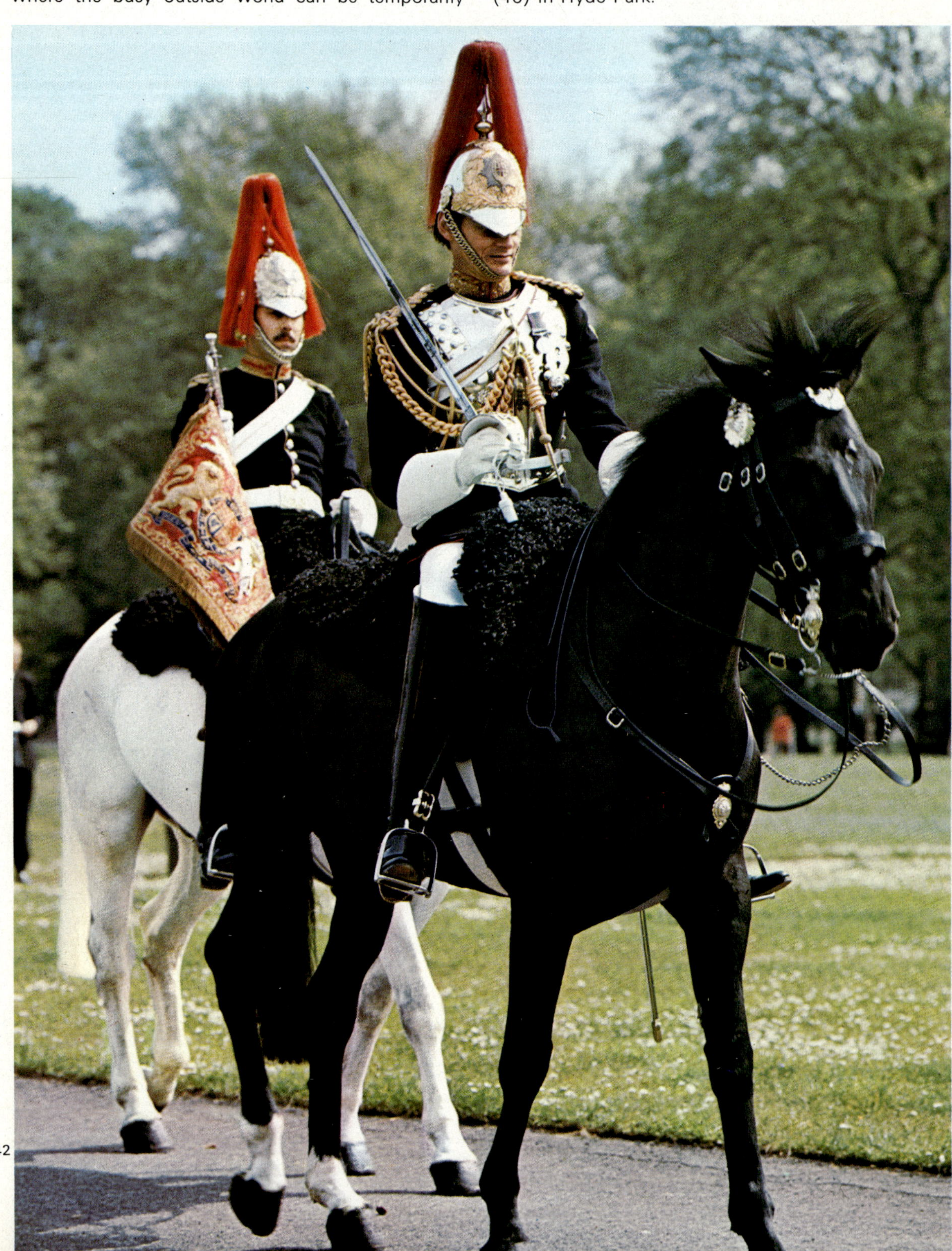

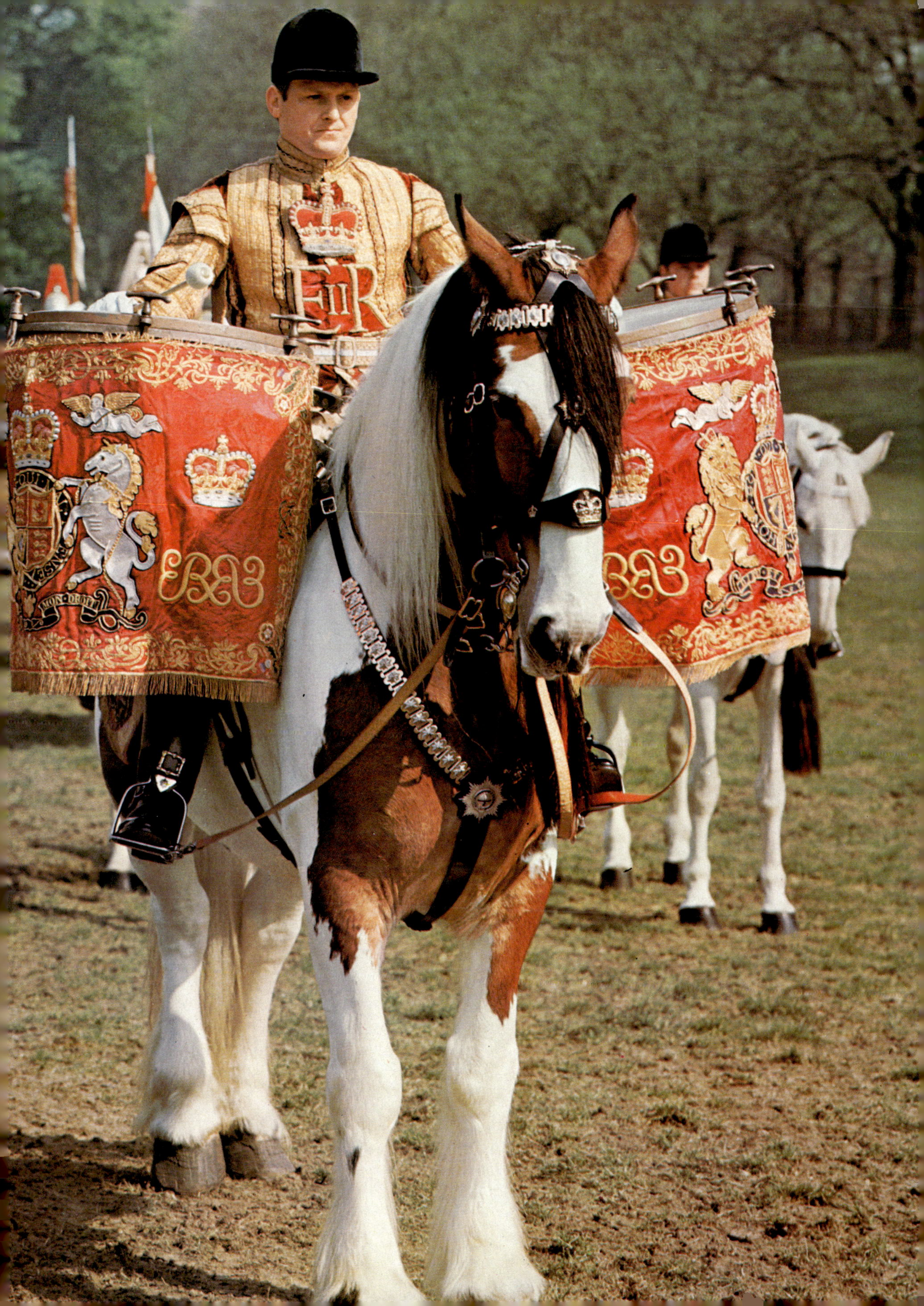

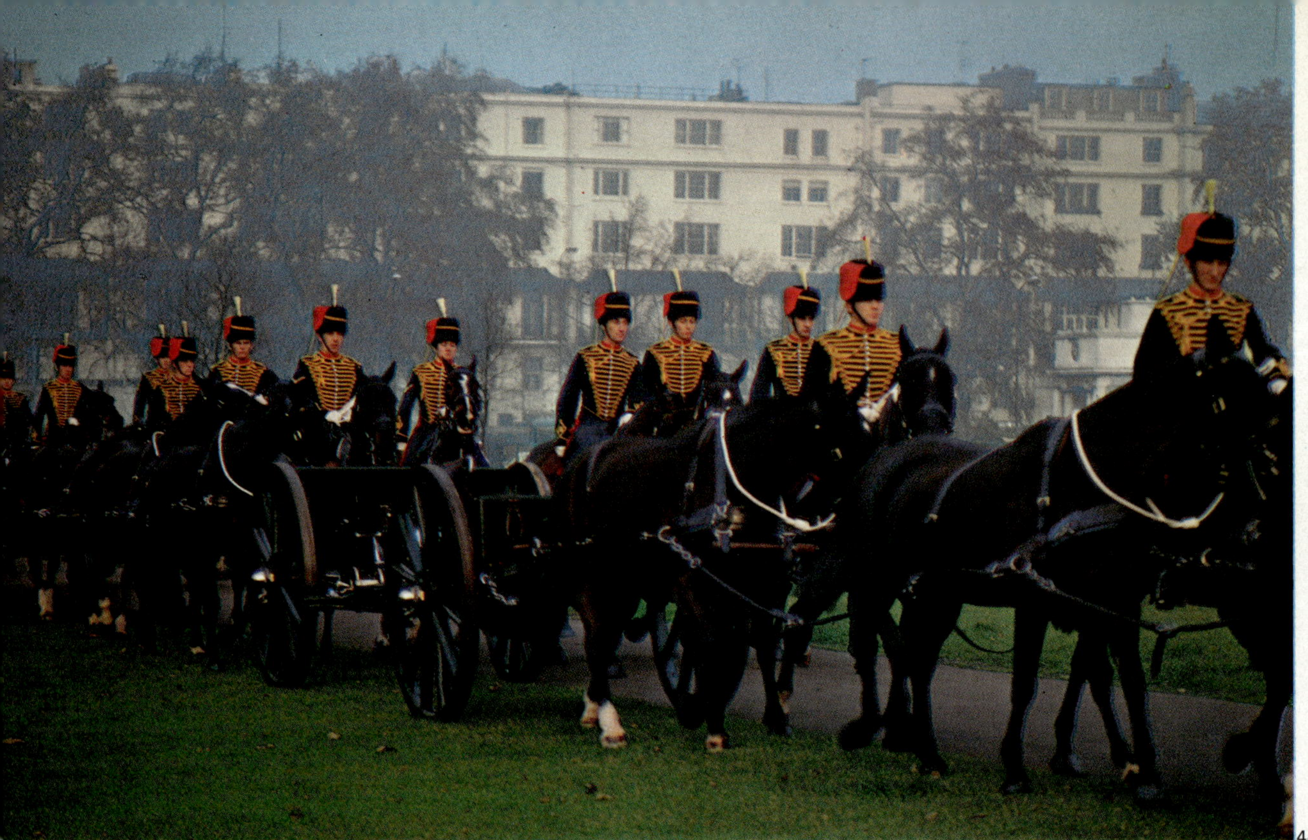

The most famous of London's many open spaces are the five Royal Parks — Hyde Park and Kensington Gardens, Regent's Park, Green Park and St James's Park. Hyde Park, together with the adjoining Kensington Gardens, forms the largest of these parks with an area of over 600 acres. Its history goes back many centuries for it originally belonged to Westminster Abbey, until the Dissolution of the Monasteries in 1536. Henry VIII then converted the area into a Royal Deer Park for his own pleasure, but Charles I opened it to the public and the park became one of London's most fashionable resorts. Rotten Row, a sandy track south of the Serpentine, was especially popular with horse-riders and the mounting blocks can still be seen by many of the gates. In the reign of Queen Anne, however, Hyde Park became a notorious haunt of both duellists and thieves, though these eventually died out and people could walk safely through the park again. The Regent's Fête was held here in 1814 in honour of the Centenary of the House of Hanover on the British throne, and celebrations after the Battle of Waterloo also took place here. Then, in 1851, the Great International Exhibition was staged in Hyde Park in the superbly designed building known as the Crystal Palace, which was later moved to Sydenham. In one corner of the park is Speaker's Corner where, on Sunday afternoons, people can air their views publicly. Beyond the Serpentine is the Bandstand, where excellent concerts are sometimes given during the summer. At 12 noon, on special occasions such as the Opening of Parliament or the Queen's Birthday, gun salutes are fired from Hyde Park by the King's Troop of the Royal Horse Artillery (44). Regent's Park, 412 acres, was laid out by John Nash and was named after the Prince Regent. This was also once a royal hunting ground but today the extremely attractive park is best known for its Zoological Gardens, founded in 1826, which are probably the finest in the world. There is also an open-air theatre in the park, which has proved very popular in the summer. Every year on Easter Monday, people flock to Regent's Park to watch the Harness Horse (or Cart Horse) Parade, when these magnificent horses, so rarely seen in London nowadays, are put through their paces (46). The old conveyances exhibited in this parade make a welcome change from the noisy, polluting traffic on the roads today. Sometimes, the Pearly Kings (45) and Queens of the London street-traders can be glimpsed in the holiday crowds. These colourful characters, resplendent in costumes which have been painstakingly decorated with tiny mother-of-pearl buttons sewn on in intricate patterns, still hold their festivals (they have their own Harvest Festival service at St Martin-in-the-Fields each October) and also do a great deal for charities. Battersea Park was originally known as Battersea Fields and was a marshy area used for vegetable-growing. In 1828, this land was purchased by the Marquess of Westminster and, between 1852 and 1858, it was converted, at great cost and labour, into a public park which today extends along the south bank of the Thames from Chelsea Bridge to Albert Bridge and comprises over 200 acres. During the celebrations of the Festival of Britain in 1951, part of the park was laid out as Festival Pleasure Gardens. These have since been redesigned and now include a lake, a theatre, an amphitheatre and, most fascinating of all, a giant fun-fair which is open every day during spring and summer. Battersea Park is always associated with the grand Easter Parade which takes place here annually on Easter Sunday. Thousands of visitors crowd into the park then, seemingly regardless of the occasional rain-storm, to watch the carnival go by (47). Easter Bonnets are, naturally, much in evidence amongst the spectators, and the more outrageous, the better. The numerous floats and tableaux are mobile works of art which must have taken months to put together, while the magnificent costumes of those taking part in the parade gleam and sparkle in the bright spring sunlight.

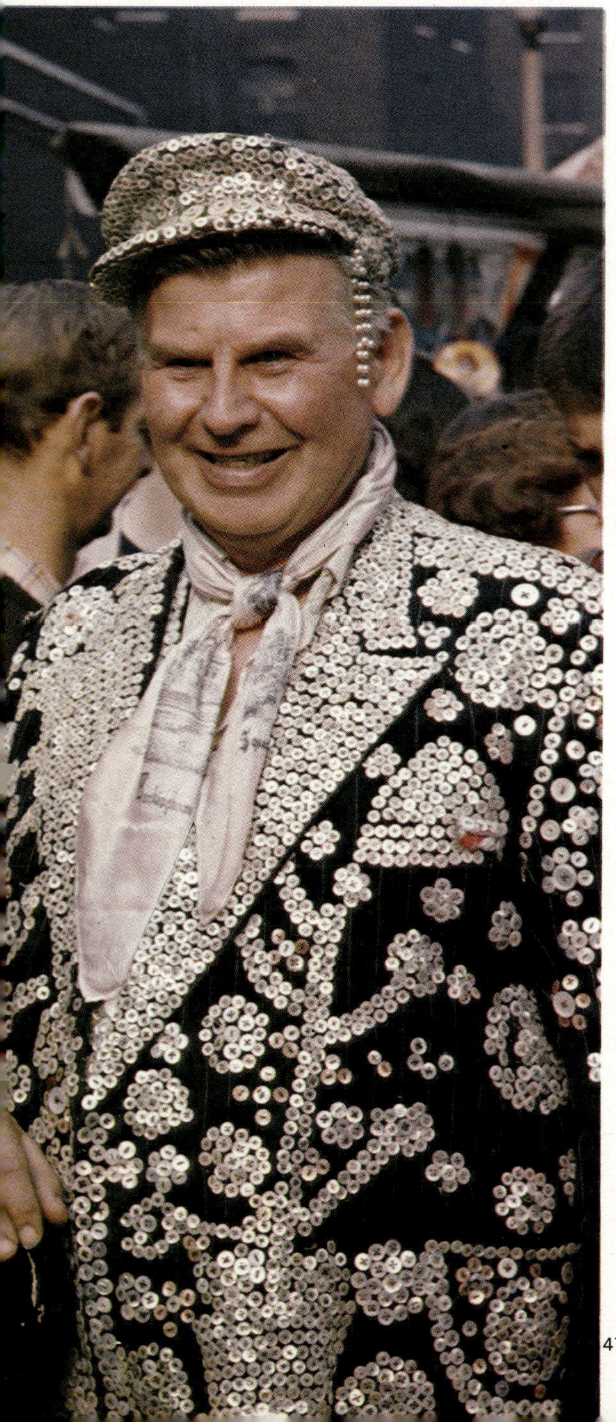

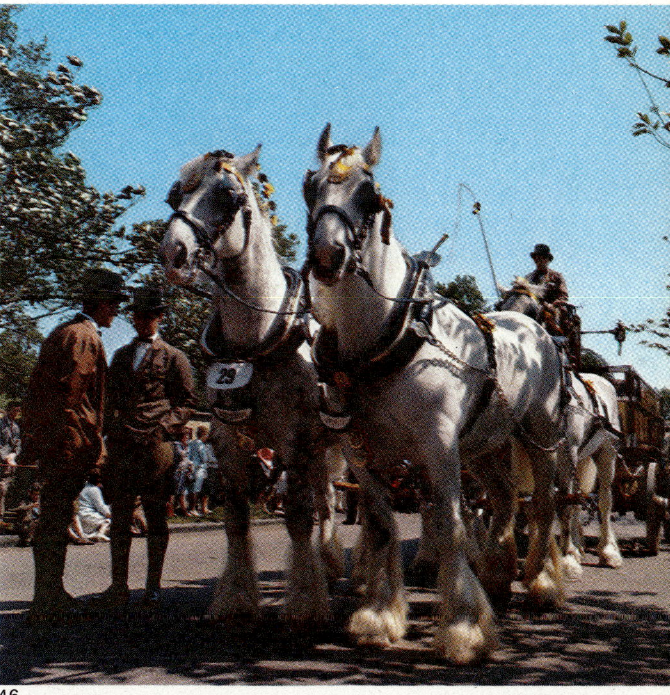

46

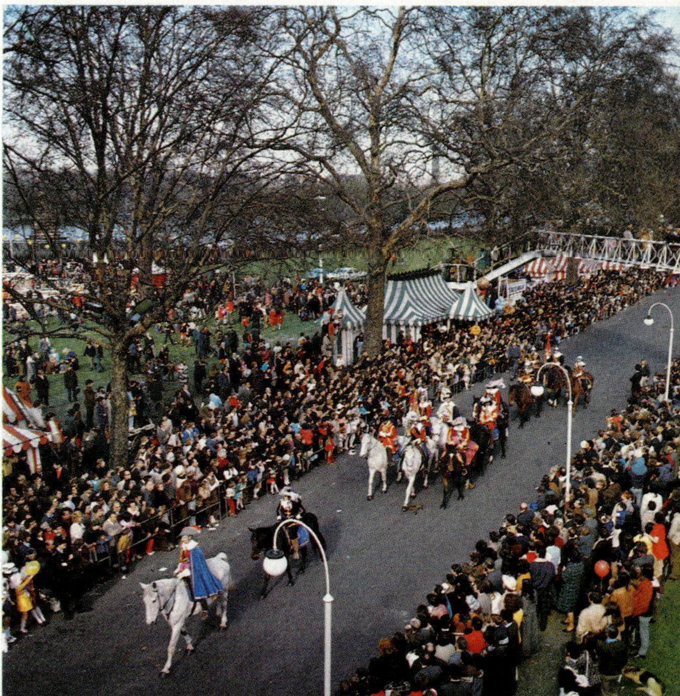

47

Windsor Castle

William the Conqueror selected Windsor (then known as Windlesora) as a strategic riverside site on which to erect a fortress after his invasion of England. His fortress was roughly built from wood and it was not till a hundred years later that the wood was replaced by stone. Since then, successive kings have altered and added to the structure but the appearance of Windsor Castle as it is today (48) owes most to the extensive restorations under Wyatville at the instigation of George IV. The Castle, which is actually the largest inhabited castle in the world, is composed of three parts: the Upper Ward, including the State Apartments, the Middle Ward with the Round Tower and the Lower Ward with St George's Chapel. The history of this chapel and the Castle itself is intrinsically bound up with the foundation of the Order of the Garter and each year in June, new knights of the Order of the Garter are invested by the Queen in Windsor Castle. After this investiture ceremony the knights, clad in full robes and insignia, walk in procession (49) to St George's Chapel for their installation.

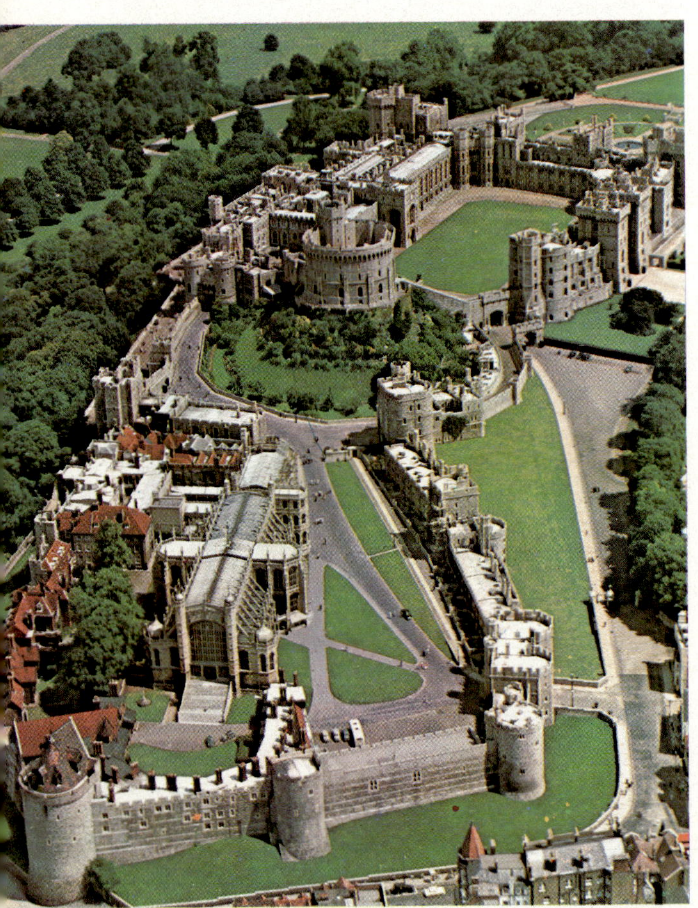

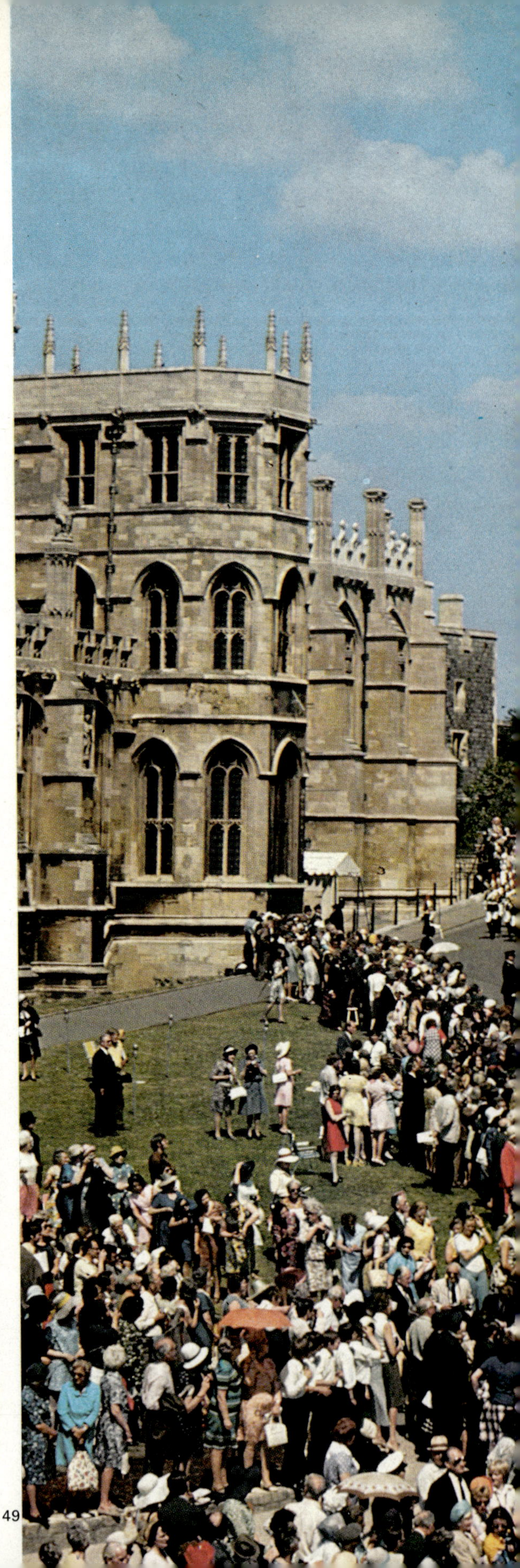

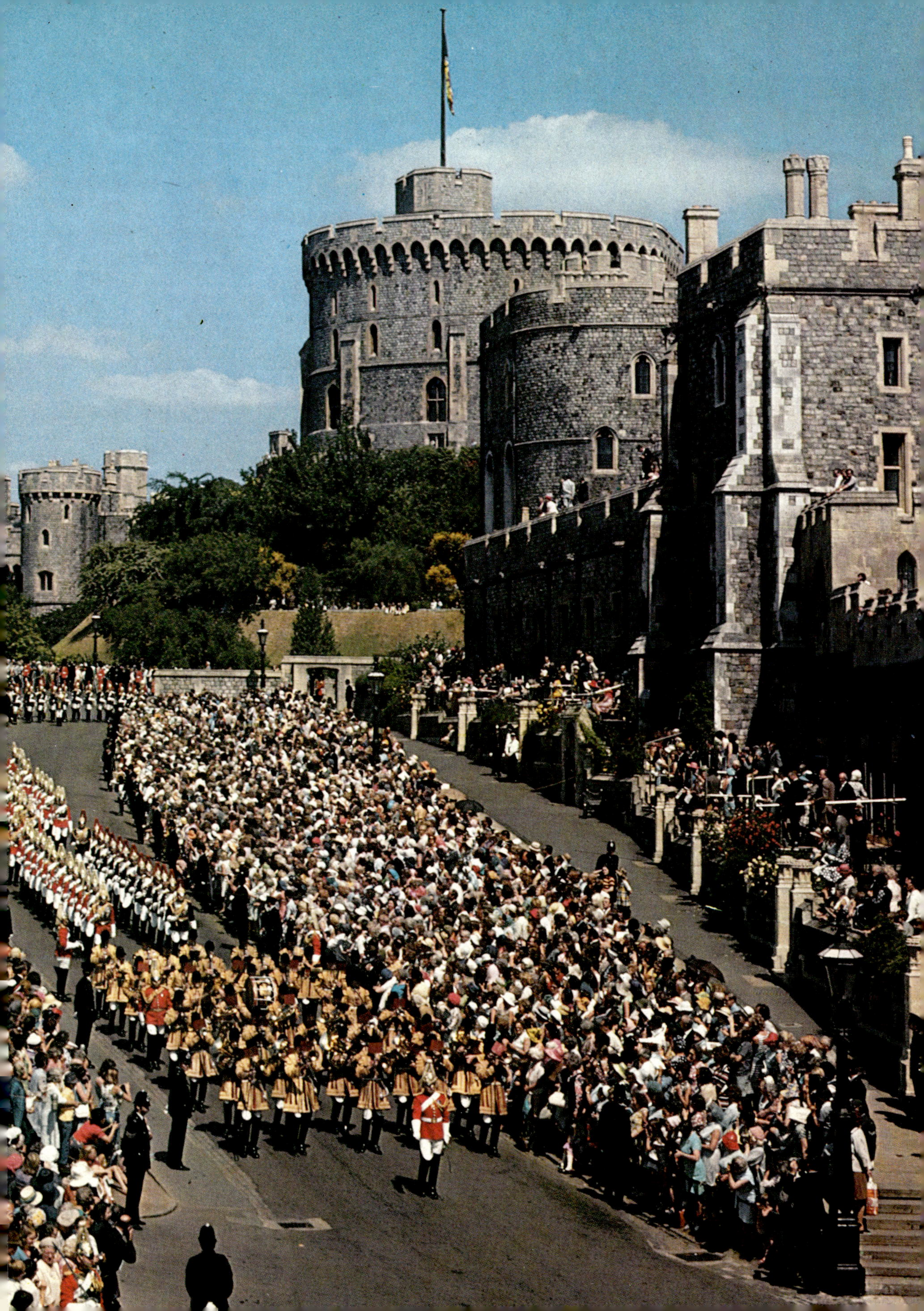

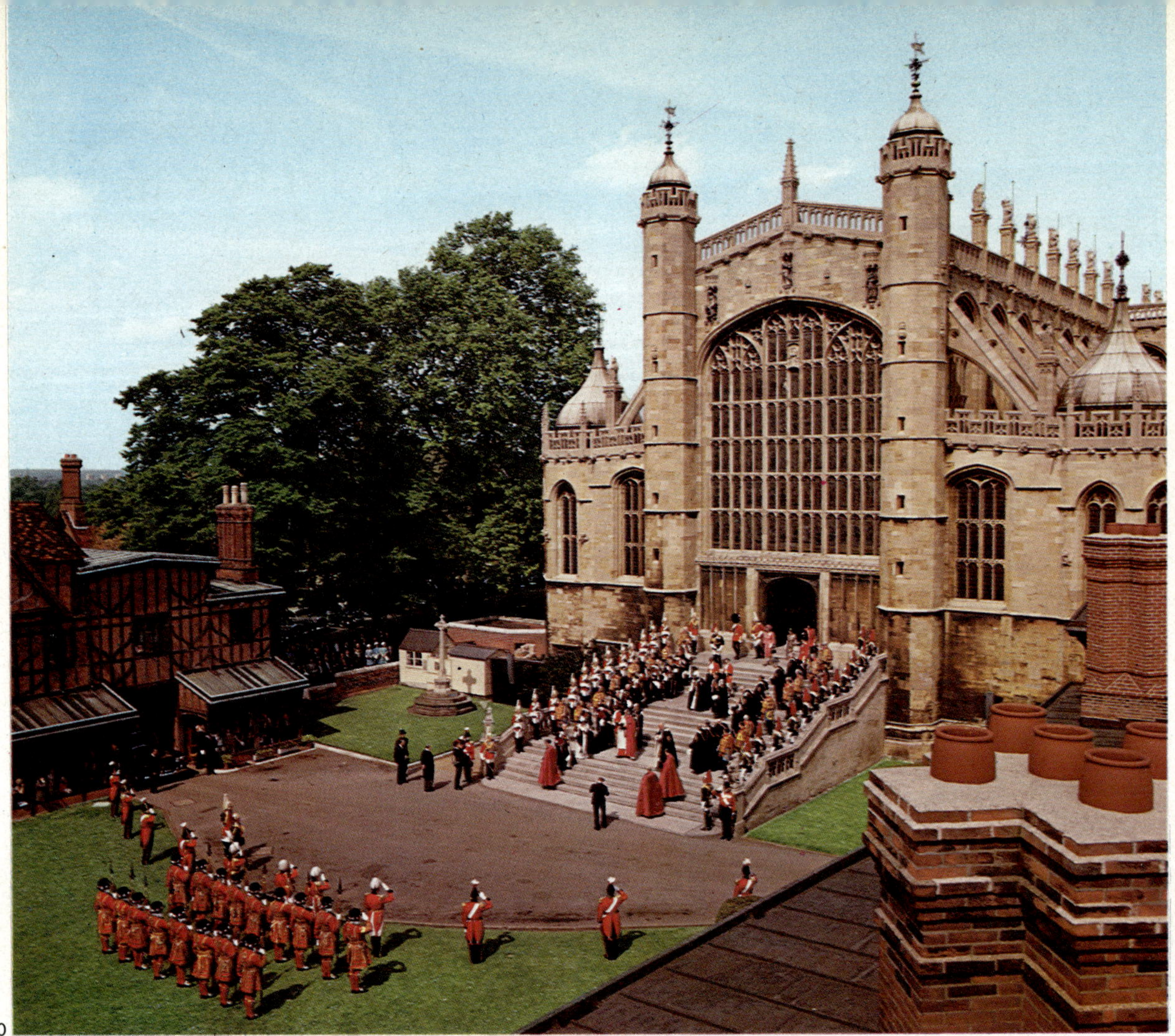

50

The Order of the Garter was founded by Edward III in the fourteenth century. Edward held a ball at Windsor and, while he was dancing with Joan, the beautiful young Countess of Salisbury, one of her garters fell to the floor. The gallant king, to save her embarrassment, immediately retrieved the offending garter and announced that he would make it famous throughout history. Thus, in 1348, he bestowed the title 'Order of the Garter' upon his knights, along with an emblem of a blue garter and the motto 'Honi soit qui mal y pense' (Shamed be he who thinks evil of it). St George's Chapel, dedicated to the Patron Saint of the Order of the Garter, was begun by King Edward IV in 1475 as a larger chapel was needed for the knights, and it was completed during the reign of King Henry VIII. It is a magnificent example of Perpendicular architecture, incorporating flying buttresses, and it is richly decorated inside with fan vaulting. Here are buried many great kings of England, including Edward IV, Henry VI, Henry VIII and Charles I. Each year, the Sovereign and Knights Companion of the Order of the Garter assemble at St George's Chapel for the formal installation (50). The stalls, which are arranged in three tiers, each bear the crests, helmets and colourful banners of the Knights of the Garter who sit there today, along with the arms of all the previous occupants of each stall.